WHO D[...]
BECO[...]

WHO DO WE BECOME?

Step boldly into our strange, new world

JOHN SANEI

Jonathan Ball Publishers
JOHANNESBURG • CAPE TOWN • LONDON

All rights reserved.
No part of this publication may be reproduced or transmitted, in any form or by any means, without prior permission from the publisher or copyright holder.

© Text John Sanei 2022
© Published edition 2022 Jonathan Ball Publishers

Originally published in South Africa in 2022 by
JONATHAN BALL PUBLISHERS
A division of Media24 (Pty) Ltd
PO Box 33977
Jeppestown
2043

ISBN 978-1-77619-216-8
ebook ISBN 978-1-77619-217-5

Every effort has been made to trace the copyright holders and to obtain their permission for the use of copyright material. The publishers apologise for any errors or omissions and would be grateful to be notified of any corrections that should be incorporated in future editions of this book.

www.jonathanball.co.za
www.twitter.com/JonathanBallPub
www.facebook.com/JonathanBallPublishers

Cover photograph by Adel Ferreira
Design and typesetting by Melanie Kriel
Cover design by John Sanei, Anita Modi Mitchell and Melanie Kriel
Set in 11/15.5pt Amasis MT

CONTENTS

INTRODUCTION 9

PART 1: ANGUISH

What happened?	16
Moving – but not *moving*	20
A rupture in meaning-making	21
I was the loneliest I had ever been	25
Being alone with loneliness is tough	26
I needed to take steps	27
Dealing with grief and loss	29
We need a moment	30
Let me tell you about when Frank died	31
Masking up	34
Let the beast sit at the table	35
The courage to change	36
The gift in adversity	37
The problem with the now	39
Responsibility for our unaware perspectives	40
From the personal to the public	43
The tyranny of comfort	45
It's just you	48

PART 2: ABNORMAL

Face forward	54
When the old ways die to make way for the new	54

The saeculum	56
The saeculum and western culture	59
The Fourth Turning and change	60
'Just in time' versus 'just in case'	60
The hero's journey	63
The future of leadership	65
The future of our economies	74
The future of technology	79
The future of the workplace	93
The future of education	101
The future of food	112
The future of love	117
The future of health	119
The future of travel	121
The future of happiness	124

PART 3: ADVENTURE

Packing your mental bags towards your imagined future	144
HINDsight	144
PLAINsight	145
INsight	146
FOREsight	147
Purpose is an equation	149
The beginning of a new road map for money	169
Finding purpose in who we become	173

ABOUT THE AUTHOR **176**

INTRODUCTION

'Midlife' is one of those words that conjures all sorts of stereotypes that have to do with falling apart and acting out, but I was finding it a wonderful, fruitful time of my life.

I was nowhere near perfect – nor am I now – but by the age of 45, I was feeling pretty confident about the choices I'd made, the things I'd learnt from my mistakes, and the way in which I had furnished my life and steered my career.

Business was exciting. Travel was easy. My ideas were solid and workable. My client base was growing. My partners in business were enthusiastic. My friends and family were supportive.

I had published four books and spoken to audiences around the world.

And, despite a sharp eye forever trained on the unstable present, the problematic past and the unfathomable future – I am, after all, a futurist – I was feeling confident about who I was in this wild world.

And then 2020 happened.

I don't really need to spell it out, do I? We were all there. We all saw doors creaking or slamming shut, blinds being pulled down, shutters padlocked. We all saw our lives shrink.

If we'd never had to deal with our inner monsters before, we were suddenly doing dances with the devil we didn't have the footwork for. If we thought we'd conquered our demons, we found them sliding out from under the bed in the terrible silence of those nights in the first lockdown when things were so quiet, we could hear our streetlamps buzz and our worst fears shrieking from some abandoned part of our brains.

I'm not going to lie. None of the tools I had seemed right for the psychological job 2020 did on me. It was tough. And I had nowhere to go. Nothing to do. All my doing had come to a screeching halt. My engagements were cancelled, which meant that, on top of all the weirdness, I was stressing about whether I would ever work again.

For a few years now, dictionaries have picked a word of the year, something that will define, in a way, what that year was like for humankind. What we were all thinking about in that year. But in 2020, the Oxford Dictionary refused to pick one word because the sheer number of new concepts that had entered our language made it impossible to choose. Some dictionaries chose 'pandemic'. Others chose 'lockdown'. But Oxford released a statement saying that the new wave of words that had entered the English language could only be honoured by scale, not by picking.

We all came to bandy some of these words about as though they'd been around forever. Blursday (which described the feeling of not knowing which day of the week it was due to being cooped up at home). Flatten the curve (when last did you hear that?). Social distancing. Quarantine pod. Unprecedented.

INTRODUCTION

Isolate. Anthropause (to describe the effects on the environment when most of the world's population wasn't going out of their homes).

What a bizarre time it was.

I found it impossible to do nothing. I was forced to, but I just couldn't. So, I started to think really hard. It's a safe place for me to retreat to, this capacity to think about things, to try to connect the dots, to make sense of everything.

Who do we become, I wondered, when the rug has been pulled out from under our feet? Who do we become when the world no longer makes sense?

The fruits of all that thinking didn't just get me through the crisis I found myself in but also became the content of the book you now hold in your hands – a book that is quite literally what is inside my head, as the cover shows.

This is what I did to get myself through. In the process, the mist that had collected in my brain cleared and I was able, again, to envisage with vigour and enthusiasm.

I know that what I've learnt in the past two years will help me for the rest of my life. My hope is that you will see yourself reflected in my own journey, and that you will use the time of reading this book as a moment to consider who you will become in this new world of ours.

Who we all might become.

JOHN

PS: In a video on her website, the international speaker and author Teal Swan wrote a forecast for 2022. The following part of it resonated very strongly for me, and I want to share it with you. She says:

> In 2022, the energies in the universe are less aligned with 'challenge'. This is not to say that 2022 will not be difficult. It is to say that 2022 provides a wave for creating and attracting what you want. In fact, so much so, that nothing is too insane or too 'out there' or too lofty to become reality. Chances are high that you felt like you were being prevented for a while. Or that everything was in your way and acting against you attracting or creating what you want in your life. That oppositional energy is clearing up in 2022. This is a year to break limitations. In 2022, you are likely to see the results of what you've been struggling to create or attract in previous years.

I have to say that, just before this, my fifth book, goes to press in the first half of 2022, I found this message incredibly reassuring and just right for the point I've reached after two years of intense self-searching.

May the things that have stood in our way for two years fall away now as we step into who we will become.

ANGUISH
AN
ANGUIS
UISH

PART 1: ANGUISH

WHAT HAPPENED?

Hindsight, the saying goes, is 20/20.

If 'hindsight' is 'understanding of a past event', and '20/20 vision' means 'perfect sight', is it possible, now, for us to fully grasp what the year 2020 meant? For nations, for business, for the environment, for wealth, for poverty, and for social and political structures?

Do *you* fully understand yet the changes that came to your life in 2020 and what those have meant for your future?

A century after the brief hiatus between the two world wars that fundamentally changed everything in the world, historians, academics and politicians are still piecing together the events that led to the destruction of entire ways of being and the loss of millions of lives. They're still trying to connect how we live now to what happened then.

How, then, can we even contemplate beginning to understand the magnitude of what has happened to us – to each and every one of the 7 753 000 000 (that's seven-point-seven billion!) of us who is still lucky enough to wake up every morning – less than a handful of years after the countries of the world started blocking their borders and ordering their citizens to stay inside in an attempt to contain the spread of the coronavirus?

Some of us have begun to adapt. Others are still floundering in the newness. Some have turned the changes into fuel for a free-floating anger so hot it has scorched not just those around them and all their social media connections but is slowly turning the person they once were to ash in the fire of their indignation. Some have collapsed into themselves, slumping through the endless days in an unrecognisable world and a paralysed stupor.

We have all lost something. We are all grieving. And the burden of pandemic grief cannot be lightened because someone else is grieving too. Grief, by definition, is an intensely lonely and individual journey. And while it has been widely observed and studied, there is no blueprint for how it is experienced. Grief lies deep in our subconscious. It lingers in the DNA of everything we do not know about ourselves.

That is why there cannot be a plan for grief. It catches us when we least expect it. For hours we forget our loss and then in the turn of a second find ourselves in the pit of the deepest despair without knowing what triggered it. When we face the deepest hopelessness and blackness, we are the only ones who can dig ourselves out. The only thing anyone else, even those closest, can share is, 'I know how you feel.' That is it. This might ease the pain, but does not take it away. It does not make it any easier to know that we're all in this together, because we are not.

My grief, your grief, and the grief of those globally has variables; it is relative. Whereas some have lost loved ones, others have lost businesses, income, or staff. People have lost their homes, have had to move in with their families or downscale, or even, frighteningly, ended up sleeping rough – in their cars, if they still have them, or in the open.

Economies have collapsed, leaders have faltered and fallen, and the work landscape has changed beyond comprehension. Even those who have lost nothing tangible have experienced loss, either vicariously, through the losses experienced by people in their lives, or through the simple fact that the framework we once used for understanding the world has collapsed or is collapsing.

As a result of this deeply unexpected and fundamentally harrowing historic event, we have lost what the Germans call 'Die Leichtigkeit' – our lightness of being.

Lightness can be maintained when we can keep at bay any thoughts we might have about the ends of things – lives, relationships, income streams – or when we have wrestled intellectually with the basic unpredictability of life and have planned within the framework of the reasonably 'knowable' in order to seek the lives we want for ourselves.

But the virus ripped that carpet out from under us.

Adversity can happen from the death of a loved one, from being diagnosed with a terminal illness or losing our business. We are conditioned, up to a point, to expect adversity. We consciously know it exists. In a way, this means we have built-in immunity to adversity. A loved one can be killed in a car accident or murdered, for example, and while this is shocking and enormously tragic, we know that things like this *can* happen.

But *this* disaster, this anguish and hardship, has struck us from nowhere and has hit us at our core. If two years ago I'd asked you if you could imagine that the world would come to a crashing halt and that the fallout would be as catastrophic, you'd have said not a chance. It was unimaginable to most. It existed only in the realm of dystopian novels and blockbuster disaster movies.

Through loss of our lightness of being, our foundation of belief no longer exists. The questions we are asking ourselves are about certainty. How can we ever trust our view of the world again? Is there ever going to be a limit on how bad things can get? How can we move forward from this space and where are we moving to? What does the future look like?

We've survived everything that has come before but now we're in the wilderness without a map or compass. Also, 'the bad' is not ending. It's grinding on and on, with wave after wave after wave. Will it ever end?

There is collective grieving, or mass trauma as it's now being called, but essentially the experience of this devastation is unique for every human being on this planet. We can share something common, but the way we live through it and experience it belongs to each of us as individuals. Everyone has experienced the pandemic differently, depending on their unique circumstances, and it's completely normal to struggle sometimes and flourish at other times.

MOVING – BUT NOT *MOVING*

I'd been living and working in Dubai for about a year when the pandemic hit. When I saw Italy and then Spain go into lockdown, I decided to move back to South Africa. The time between the decision and being back on the family farm in Magoebaskloof was about twenty-four hours. A few months later I moved to Cape Town, where I'd been staying a few years before I went to Dubai.

It was a lot of moving – but very little moved. It was as though life was proceeding at the pace of a feature film in slow motion.

As I sat in the confines of my four walls, trying to rebuild my career, I was aware of the stark contrast between my life and the one I'd been living two years earlier. From jetting around the world and drawing energy from connecting with an audience on stage, I was now all alone, with nowhere to go.

Sadness, I think, is a breakdown of momentum. I had been stopped in my tracks. We had all been denied – quite literally, by lockdown – the ability to move. I think many of us had a new sense of what exactly the word 'freedom' meant. And how 'captivity' means 'restriction of movement'.

My vision became as confined as the view from my window. As a futures strategist, I read avidly and research intensely, but I couldn't safely say what was in store for me or for the world. For the first time in my life, I had no way to puzzle together any possible long-term scenarios. I felt bereft, not only of all the things we were all losing, but of the very tools I needed for my career: my ability to imagine, envision and predict.

A RUPTURE IN MEANING-MAKING

Nothing really made sense any more. Getting to grips with this pandemic and its effect on me seemed impossibly daunting.

Psychologist David Trickey of the Anna Freud Centre for Children and Families in London, who is the co-director of the United Kingdom's Trauma Council, says that when the way you see yourself, the world and other people is shocked or overturned by an event, simple stress cascades into trauma through sustained and severe feelings of helplessness.

I found that even small, everyday setbacks took on the feeling of massive trauma. My personal navigation system was linked to my work and when I found myself without a single booking, my self-esteem and purpose went into a frightening freefall. The mental resilience that had always kept me moving forward despite small and big setbacks was suddenly depleted.

There was nothing external to define, evaluate and validate my worth. No matter how often I bombarded myself with the word 'why', there was no answer. I'd been on the up before the pandemic hit. Years of hard work after a rebound from bankruptcy and a scarring divorce was paying off and I was starting to gain solid international momentum, when virtually overnight my carefully crafted future shattered.

I watched friends and colleagues suffer through disease and death, without time to say farewells or to soothe their loved ones. Mourning rituals were distanced, confused and clinical.

Then there were the relentless visuals of medical tubes, healthcare workers unrecognisable in their protective gear, and council workers in hazmat suits spraying public places. There was the silence of the streets, the clarity of the air without traffic pollution. The tension wasn't imagined: it was reaching us through every sense we have for making experiential sense of the world.

And before the inevitable familiar daily tally of infections and deaths, there was this tense waiting without any real evidence about how serious the problem really was.

'Being unable to breathe is the most traumatic event you can imagine,' says Metin Başoğlu, founder of the Trauma Studies section at King's College in London. 'There is nothing you can do about it. Once you are out of breath, only helplessness can follow.' It felt as if everyone, myself included, was holding their collective breath, waiting and willing it all to end, and for life to return to normal.

I decided to try to reclaim this normalcy on my parents' farm in Magoebaskloof.

I once held strong opinions of men in their thirties and forties still living at home with their parents. Losers, I thought. And yet there I was, staying with my folks in their guesthouse. I was helping Mom change the sheets on my bed and it dawned on me that I had become the person I had always harshly judged. I had gone from a jet-setting man-about-town to being to a mommy's boy, in my forties, virtually overnight.

What we resist persists, until we make our peace with it.

It wasn't permanent, of course, and I'm grateful I could stay on their farm and spend valuable time with my mom and stepdad. But I did ask myself, more than once, whether this was what all my hard work had amounted to.

Community and social connection are essential for getting through difficulty, but the lockdowns denied us the very thing we needed to cope because we understood that moving about could spread the virus and we really wanted the virus to stop spreading.

Everyone had to scramble to make sense of their new working lives and fast-track to the remote office with all its seemingly insurmountable problems, like how to keep the animals and children off the screen during meetings without losing your cool in front of colleagues.

Like millions of others, my office was my home. I put up two pictures behind me – one of a magnificent white owl, symbolising wisdom, the other of a protea to embody blossoming ideas. They might look good when I'm in meetings, but they did nothing to help me fast-track my sudden need to learn about Zoom and generally fast-track my grasp on technology.

I had my fair share of flops. Like the time I had to pivot from being on a stage to presenting an online conference for 800 Abu Dhabi government staff members. Being the guy who speaks about the future, you are expected to be in control of all 'future' stuff too, but here I was, battling to get my slides to work. I was there to give them hope – all I can say for certain that I taught them was patience.

I did come to realise that Microsoft Teams was not a friendly system when using a Mac and cracked up when I saw a meme that felt it had been written for me: 'When I receive a Teams invite I see it as a sign of aggression.'

These disconnects did little to help boost my mastery of this tech world I suddenly found myself immersed in.

And at the end of days like those, there was not a soul around for me to vent to, debrief with or cry-laugh with about my embarrassment and frustration. This detachment amplified my anguish severalfold. I was yearning for the normalcy of preparing for work, connecting face to face with other people and exchanging energy.

Everything that had given my life meaning – that had given me my sense of myself within a network of people and organisations, the work that had given me both purpose and self-esteem – had been jumbled and I felt like I was in free fall.

For some people, the changed world immediately offered new purpose and vigour, but I would argue that, for most people, it was one of the most extreme ruptures of meaning-making they had ever experienced.

I WAS THE LONELIEST I HAD EVER BEEN

Many years ago, I worked with Oneness University from India and one of the processes they initiated with us was to sit with our emotions and really feel them. Not just the good ones, but the uncomfortable, the troubling and the overwhelming ones.

The idea is that the feelings will only pass after we've befriended them. When we ignore our emotions, or push them away, they haunt us until they are heard, felt and integrated. Feelings are fleeting when we allow ourselves to feel them. For us to exist fully means to assimilate both joy and pain, togetherness and loneliness.

I absorbed this lesson then. Now, I had been given an opportunity to put this discipline to the test for loneliness.

Because for someone whose entire being is centred on being with others – learning from and laughing with, liking and loving – being alone in my home was proving to be a trial I wasn't fully equipped for.

We've been raised to believe that loneliness is not sexy, not desirable. That it's pitiful to be alone. We're conditioned into thinking we should be with someone, with anyone, or everyone – as long as we're not alone. We continuously seek the salve of relation by counting likes, moulding ourselves towards trends and hashtags. We seek validation from the outside. Being alone is regarded as peculiar or embarrassing or even unhealthy.

I know that there is a slight – but massive – shift in perspective to differentiate between whether what you're feeling is loneliness or solitude, and I'm usually really good at knowing the difference. But given this amount of change and grief, I could not stave off falling into a pit of loneliness. When grief and anguish comes over me, I am intensely lonely.

BEING ALONE WITH LONELINESS IS TOUGH

The seventeenth-century writer and mathematician Blaise Pascal said: 'All man's miseries derive from not being able to sit quietly in a room alone.'

Solitude is necessary for our well-being and potential

success. It is the key to higher self-awareness, which opens the door to change. As Sheryl Sandberg, chief operating officer of Meta Platforms, Inc. (Facebook) and the founder of LeanIn.Org, says: 'We cannot change what we are not aware of and once we are aware, we cannot help but change.'

Forced as I was to face my loneliness on my own, I had to start thinking about the difference between the connotations of solitude and the negative feelings I had about being alone. Author Amy Morin describes it best when she says: 'Loneliness is about perceiving that no one is there for you. But solitude is about making a choice to be alone.'

I hadn't made the choice to be alone. It had been thrust on me. It was unwelcome and uncomfortable. It chafed. Being, as I am, constantly connected socially, being linked has become a drive that keeps me moving forwards. It is the source of my energy and my creativity.

My first instinct was to rebuild my world, but my creativity was gone. Access to what feeds me had been cut off.

I discovered that it's not easy to sit alone with your thoughts for extended periods.

I NEEDED TO TAKE STEPS

I knew, theoretically, that unplugging for the sake of my mental health was critical and that spending time alone was a way to unleash innovative thinking, but hell, it was hard.

As luck would have it, I befriended my neighbour's dog, Bean, and started taking her for walks. I upped my exercise routine, deciding to train for an Ironman Triathlon to give myself a sense of control over something in my life, and this process taught me to change my relationship with pain – which was not what I was expecting to learn, but which came in handy.

What I was trying to do was build the habit of embracing solitude and, by so doing, I invited more into life. Taking walks with Bean gave me purpose and a connection, and she became, in a way, my study partner, as this is when I listened to lectures on my headphones about our emerging world – something I didn't have time for before COVID.

What was happening was a process of positive disintegration, though it didn't necessarily always feel positive. Things were being sloughed off me and the bits left behind were feeling raw and vulnerable. But I started to see that perhaps the things I was losing were aspects of myself I no longer needed. I was finding the raw and vulnerable parts suddenly revealing. Useful, even.

I started to go into the feeling of loneliness the way I had been taught. It was no longer theoretical. It had become a practical exercise in learning to make of the moment the best that I could, no matter how much my spirit rebelled against the forced newness of my life. I had spoken about difficulty on stage. I had acknowledged it existed and that it could be overcome. Now, I was personally up against something I was finding very difficult.

Isolation meant embracing solitude and, I'm not going to lie, hard as I worked at it, there were moments of deep loneliness and terrible despair.

DEALING WITH GRIEF AND LOSS

Most of us spent the first few months of the pandemic – perhaps we still are – simply coping. Working harder, or differently, in changed circumstances. We've been trying to help those who were losing their livelihoods, or those without homes or food, while contemplating our own possibly diminished financial futures. We were working on our relationships in new ways, watching people we love burn out, or crash, or retreat into a deep darkness, not knowing what to say or do to make anything better for them. All of this while we ourselves were trying not to crash or burn or disappear into a well of sadness and overwhelm.

Let's be frank: we've not had a moment to process the implications of the pandemic. There has been neither the space nor the time to deal consciously with our grief about the many things we've lost.

WE NEED A MOMENT

A friend, Adrian McKenna, was once sitting by a body of water doing nothing but observing – a rare and valuable thing that we seldom seem to have time for. Not reading, or talking, or scrolling or even thinking very deeply, but just sitting quietly and experiencing the pleasure of the senses.

After a while, he realised that as long as the water rippled, he was unaware of the trees and clouds reflected on its surface. As soon as the water came to absolute stillness, the surface acted as a mirror. 'There is no reflection without stillness,' he told me, a sentence that stayed with me, and whose deep intelligence I only really came to understand during that time of loneliness and suffering.

The more we suppress it – in order to do what we need to do to get through – the more we run the risk of having sorrow sneak up on us unexpectedly. It sits deep within us, waiting to be released. You're doing something simple, mundane, and you look up and suddenly the entire spectrum of loss, longing and sadness washes over you. There is such fragility in this, amplifying the feelings of powerlessness and helplessness.

It can really unbalance you when this happens. Isn't it so much easier to control the effect of those emotions, if you are quietly sitting and purposefully inviting reflection on them? They can't knock you over when you are sitting. They can unsettle you, but they're less likely to hurl you across the room.

It is the pinnacle of irony, I have found, that when I allow myself to positively disintegrate, release my identity, forget who I thought I was and trust the process of becoming who I need to be, I find my way towards myself.

'The only way to relax with yourself is to open your heart,' writes Chögyam Trungpa Rinpoche in 'Facing Yourself', a chapter in a book called *Smile at Fear*. 'Then you have a chance to see who you are. This experience is like opening a parachute. When you jump out of an airplane and open the chute, you are there in the sky by yourself. Sometimes it is very frightening, but on the other hand, when you take this step, the whole situation, the whole journey, makes sense. You have to actually do it, and then you will understand.'

LET ME TELL YOU ABOUT WHEN FRANK DIED

Frank was like a father to me and when he died. I felt as though I had lost something as fundamental. I felt bereft.

Frank was the father of a friend of mine and embodied an idea of manhood, which now might seem antiquated and curious, but which had a positive influence on many young men. It was only at his funeral that I realised that the profound effect he had on my life was multiplied several times over in the effect he'd had on other people's lives. He made me feel seen and special. The fact that he'd had that effect on several other people attests to the largeness of the man's life and his spirit.

I am the oldest of two boys and my mother was a single mother. She provided and protected us with the energy and vigour of many dedicated parents, but she could not be the thing I didn't even realise I craved: a father.

Frank was Irish, a welder and a sailor, who'd come to South Africa on a ship and ended up making a life here. He was a big, well-built man, a bodybuilder, a sport, and he inspired in me an appreciation of my body's capabilities and my mind's ability to be honed and trained. He was an unpretentious man, who ran a small but very successful company with two employees, and he dished out love and lessons in the same unpretentious way. He would tell us stories, recite poems to us, this big, burly, gruff alpha male. It was from his lips that I first heard the poem 'Invictus' by William Ernest Henley, which ends with the words 'I am the captain of my soul'.

This is what Frank gave me: a sense of my own agency, the power to make the right decisions, and the ways in which to make doing the right thing easier. Here's an example. He was the first person to tell me how important it was to drink green juice. I complained that I knew it was important, but that I found it such a schlepp to clean the juicer that I couldn't be bothered. He said: 'Make it a ritual.'

He explained to me how he welcomed the job of cleaning

the juicer as part of the ritual of self-care. He turned something that seemed unpleasant to me into something not just tolerable, but welcome.

I was 40 when he died and his death hit me hard. I was devastated, but I had no idea how to grieve. I was deeply moved to be asked to be the speaker at his funeral, which was attended by hundreds of people. But that didn't help the sense of loss.

There was a recurrent underlying niggling question: what if what I needed was to get comfortable with this loss? I chose to mourn consciously. In fact, I did my best to *enjoy* the mourning because it felt like a celebration of a man I had admired and loved. It was also an opportunity to go deeper into my heart and to heal other aspects of my sorrow. Frank's passing turned out to be, in essence, a gateway to many uncried cries and unsobbed sobs.

This, I realise now, was preparation for the strangeness that was coming – an opportunity to become more familiar with dealing with adversity. Consciously mourning Frank was groundwork for the grief of 2020.

Dealing with the passing of Frank and doing a deep dive into my pandemic-induced sadness did not stall or arrest misery. It hasn't eradicated twinges of anguish and bouts of melancholy. What it has done is help me feel at ease with these feelings.

And once I can be with the feelings without trying to duck and dive or fight them, I try to replace sadness with happy memories. I give myself a positivity painkiller by reminding myself about this wonderful life of memories I had before COVID-19. This helps me pass more easily through this instant of grief. I've found this part necessary, or the grief would threaten to swallow me up. It could engulf me. Choke me. It would literally take my breath away with its ferocity.

Then, when the time and place and space is right, I do it all over again. I sit with these emotions, and I offer them the olive branch.

MASKING UP

Masks will from now on, and for a very long time, be a symbol of a specific time in our lives, and also an image of what divides us. Masks have not only divided us into those who believe in their efficacy to protect them and those who feel they impinge on their freedoms, but also, perhaps, between our inner and outer selves, our private and social selves.

Masks have become mandatory in our lives to hamper the spread of the virus. But masks also mean that we have licence not to put on a brave face, not to fake smiles and not to engage in small talk.

It's hard to have conversation – sometimes it's even hard

to recognise someone – with our masks on. Our easy-breezy culture of 'How are you? Fine, thanks, and you?' has mostly now been reduced because the masks make it even harder to find connection in casual encounters than ever before.

On the other hand, the mask gives us permission to not be fine. It allows us to be silent too. In silence, the tough emotions rise to the surface. In a culture that prefers to turn grief away at the door, we are now required to entertain it in our homes.

LET THE BEAST SIT AT THE TABLE

At home, in stillness, in a state of shock or panic or despair, with our inner resources all but depleted, it makes sense to simply allow grief in when it arrives, instead of trying to banish it. To sit down with the grief at your table and entertain it. *Properly*, not reluctantly. In the same way that I embraced actively mourning Frank, perhaps there are lessons from breaking bread with the beast.

As the writer James Baldwin so powerfully put it, not everything that is faced can be changed, but nothing can be changed until it is faced. His words can be applied to almost anything, from enormous social and political stumbling blocks like institutional racism and misogyny to the simplest behavioural changes we desire within ourselves.

With the beast of grief at our table, perhaps we could make a list of all that we feel we have lost and then make a list of all that we feel we might have gained. It is human to focus on the ways in which we feel we or others have failed, forgetting entirely about that which we and others have done well, or overcome, or achieved in the face of adversity.

THE COURAGE TO CHANGE

Armed with a new consciousness, then, our next question is, are we courageous enough to change? Let me tell you something about myself. It requires me to reveal an aspect of myself that I'm not proud of, but I hope it will demonstrate what I mean.

I am successful. I have friends who are more successful and so within my group we have billionaires and although money isn't the only way to measure success, it's a powerful one and I had a deep, deep envy about it.

I had to seek counsel. I had to go for healing and I did many sessions about envy and now I feel so released of it.

To truly celebrate the success of somebody else so close to you, and to give yourself the permission to achieve that same kind of success, is such a gift. But for 25 years, I had quietly, secretly and in my own head been envious of people who were more successful than me.

When I speak to people about it now, they sheepishly say, yes, me too. We don't want to talk about this openly. It's embarrassing.

Because envy is the antithesis of gratefulness.

The question is, do I sink into the warming, lulling comfort of feeling sorry for myself, because that's what feels familiar, and then blame fifteen things for why I don't have something that someone else has? Or do I take my focus and say, I don't like that. It doesn't make me feel energised. I don't want to take this into the future with me. I actually want to celebrate my friends. Seek help.

The courage to change always benefits us if we are people who want to grow with an eye on who we will become. It's always hard, but it comes with unexpected gifts.

If the upheaval of the past few years is not enough to change us, then I think the lessons from the pandemic have been lost on us. If it doesn't bring about better beings, better systems, and a better world, then it has been wasted on humankind.

THE GIFT IN ADVERSITY

The author Rabbi Harold Kushner, reflecting on the death of his son, said in an article: 'I am a more sensitive person, a more effective pastor, a more sympathetic counsellor because of Aaron's life and death than I would ever have been without it. And I would give up all those gains in a second if I could have my son back. If I could choose I would forgo all of the spiritual growth and depth which has come my way and because of our experiences ... but I cannot choose.'

Healthy personality development often requires the disintegration of dearly held beliefs about ourselves and the world. Psychic suffering, self-doubt, depression and anxiety generally precede meaningful change. But Polish psychologist Kazimierz Dąbrowski believed this process of unravelling could lead to a deeper examination of what we could become and, ultimately, to higher levels of personality development and an increased sense of meaning in life.

Before COVID, I was all about me. I was building a global personal brand, working on becoming an influencer in the high-pressure world of social media. It was all about image and appearance; about me, myself and I. About self-promotion. Instant gratification.

Now, the shift seems to be a collective search for online heroes who are regular people, people who have overcome adversity, pain and sorrow. There are many examples of people who have stood up and moved forward from these extraordinary experiences in exemplary ways. It shows us that calamity can be overcome, and it offers us invaluable material for inspiration and hope.

THE PROBLEM WITH THE NOW

We hear repeatedly that to overcome suffering, we have to live in the present and value the moment. We're told this is the only way to deal with an uncertain future.

I would argue, though, that no one can live only in the present. Not one of us is enlightened enough to exist without hindsight and foresight as the pillars of our existence. The present can only be held up by what came before and what comes next. It is not a single domino that can stand alone. I sit here as a collective result of the history before my time and as the starting point of everything that comes tomorrow.

I must be willing to acknowledge the part I played in the past, the part I play this very instant and the part I will play in the future.

As a human being, with a timeline, I am forced to take responsibility.

Sitting down with the beast more often than not means thinking about yourself in the most truthful way you can. It means acknowledging that you are not all-knowing and all-powerful. That you have made mistakes. Taken wrong turns. Hurt people, whether you meant to or not.

RESPONSIBILITY FOR OUR UNAWARE PERSPECTIVES

What does 'take' responsibility mean?

I hear you say, 'I've taken responsibility. I've kept a roof over our heads. I've fed my kids and paid their school fees. I'm working myself into the ground at half the salary I earned a year ago.'

You're right. And I hope you have taken some time in your silence to appreciate yourself and how hard you've worked to keep things together.

But taking responsibility is also about the ability to respond, not react.

I've had to accept that life is difficult, not only objectively but because sometimes I make it so. I have had to discover within myself the facets that connect me with every other human being – the criminal, the corrupt politician, the adulterous husband, the negligent son. All these things, in other words, that I think I am not. This 'dark matter of the me', if I can say it that way, can manifest as judgement or prejudice, biases or discrimination. And very often I am not even aware that those things are part of me. In fact, the unconscious will go out of its way to sidestep responsibility for that in me which is less than attractive.

Psychologists call this 'the superiority illusion', the idea that in any given metric, we are better than the average person. And the law of averages makes it very clear: if we are all better than average, as we believe we are, then we are all pretty average. And fallible. And prone to making terrible gaffes.

We must accept that we cannot see ourselves fully at any point, and that we are inclined to suppress that in us which we or society thinks of as 'bad' or 'inappropriate' or 'unacceptable'. And we need also to learn to take it on the chin – from ourselves and from others – when it is pointed out to us that we are wrong or that our behaviour, attitude, or language has hurt others.

Sometimes experience through adversity forces us into a situation where we can choose to acknowledge, take responsibility for and assimilate what we find distasteful about ourselves. But here's the good news: it can heal our character. It can make us better humans, friends, lovers, colleagues and citizens.

Let me share an example. One of my best friends was married to a Motswana woman. When she came to Cape Town, she remarked to me how racist she felt the people here were. I argued with her. At the time, I had no idea that my experience of the world was not her experience of the world. I am a white man. She is a black woman.

The argument bothered me, but I left it. Many years later I was on a flight and the white guy across the way from me had to get out of his aisle seat to let another white man move to the seat at the window. Pleasantries were exchanged. Moments later he had to repeat the action for a black woman. This time his face was hard and unfriendly.

I found this scenario so striking, and so deeply disturbing, that it triggered an inner dialogue. I could suddenly see something I'd not seen before. If you are not the recipient of racist behaviour, it can seem like a subtle, vague worry. But suddenly, the true, ugly nature of quiet, everyday racism revealed itself to me in the face of this man. Suddenly, I could see what my friend's wife had been telling me.

It wasn't pleasant to discover this about myself. My sense of myself does not correlate with someone who is insensitive and thoughtless or who brushes off other people's experience of the world.

I was not aware of my prejudices, masculine dominance, or misogyny until recent years. I continue to learn. Realising just how blinded I have been to some of my own preconceived ideas was astounding to me, even more so as I slowly peel away the layers of this unaware perspective.

I must accept responsibility for even those things that operated beneath the level of my consciousness. For the shadows lurking in the depths. How can I become better at this thing called living, at being human, if I refuse to acknowledge my blind spots and weaknesses?

In a very touching message to the matriculants of 2021, the wise Lwando Xaso, whose Instagram feed is full of useful observations about society, wrote: 'An indication of our progress is our ability to fail and make mistakes and not have those failures or mistakes have the final say on who we are … Don't be driven by a fear of failure. Failure is valuable information. Instead, be driven by the inspiration of what you have to offer the world. And remember you are alchemists; you can spin magic out of what the world perceives as failure.'

It's not just young people who need to comprehend this, though. Being kind to ourselves when we fail, or for past failures, frees us to do the learning that mistakes require of us.

FROM THE PERSONAL TO THE PUBLIC

It is an immensely painful process to see yourself beyond the superiority illusion, to assimilate what is less attractive into your sense of self, without shame. Yet it confirms the oneness and interrelatedness of being. It dissolves judgement.

Just because I have identified this, though, doesn't mean I'll act on it. It means that because I am conscious of what I am capable of, I can make a conscious choice to act or not act. This is what makes me feel as though I am taking responsibility.

An altered perspective can shift us. More important, though, is that these changed views are tooled into a collective shift in consciousness and responsibility. Epiphany can evolve from the life that language takes on in an exchange of millions of brains coming together. If we collectively say something, then feel something, then change something, we are learning to heal and master ourselves.

Feelings are reactive, but being conscious of the power of my emotions I can feel angry but choose not to act on it immediately. It doesn't change my feeling – it changes the outcome. It means that I know my triggers, and that I can learn that I am my response.

We are living in a time when people who have never had voices before are being heard. They are telling us about their pain, the pain of their parents, the pain of generations of people who have been sidelined and overlooked at best, and impeded, harassed and harmed at worst. Whatever those people are saying, we must listen and learn to modulate our reactions. We need to respond with sensitivity, not defensiveness. We need to learn to sit with the beast, without wanting to shoo it away, diminish it or deny it.

Whether the grief we allow in is our own, or a group's, or a collective's, we need to give it space at our table, allow ourselves to feel our feelings, and then make thoughtful choices about how to move into the future.

So, the question I've been asking myself is what opportunity has been presented to me by being stripped of my beliefs through loss and grief, brought about by this seismic shift in our world since the virus reared its ugly head?

I can feel angry and hopeless, but by choosing to act on that am I forsaking my own evolution? What I can do is rise to the challenge of getting to know myself better, to hopefully become a better human being?

I think that within that answer the pandemic serves a purpose greater than myself.

Accepting all my own idiosyncrasies has brought great relief through this giant grief I have experienced. More of me is in the room. More of me is present to say, 'This is who I am.' And I am okay with who I am. I'm going to be better friends with you, John. This has been a rewarding process.

THE TYRANNY OF COMFORT

While grief is intensely personal, we are all on the same planet and we have a collective responsibility to do better than we have in the past. That's what progress is. Learning in a thoughtful, voluntary, and goal-directed way. We have caused immeasurable damage to one another, to ourselves and to the earth. More damage could be done if we do not step up and be better than we've ever been before.

Suffering is not a journey; it should be a tool. Adversity is not a journey; it should be a tool. They are the latchkeys to unlocking a future that is vastly different, more inclusive, and more collaborative than our past.

If we can understand our suffering as not being a special and unique torture aimed specifically and personally at us, if we can appreciate suffering as a gift rather than victimisation, it will open the gateway to our greater purpose.

Purpose is healed pain that comes from the heart, not the head.

To make purpose of pain, however, requires us to pay attention to it. Adversity, suffering, pain and grief can bring about transformative consciousness. Sipping piña coladas on the beach day in, day out is not going to bring about much growth. Neither will living a conditioned, comfortable life, or glossing over, ignoring, or shutting down our distress or discomfort.

Pain is hard work. It asks every inch of who and what we are.

We strive to make our lives as physically, emotionally and mentally comfortable as possible. We order takeaways rather than cook. Throw all our rubbish in one black bag, instead of sorting out the recyclables. Use words we're comfortable with without asking what their effect is on others. Accept antidepressants after a brief visit to our overstretched GP instead of dealing with our issues.

Ease is great, but it doesn't allow for much growth. Comfort is a tyranny. If we accept that – if we prefer progress over stagnation and growth over statis – we must rethink our relationship with pain, developing confidence in our physical and emotional ability to change and our hunger and aptitude for learning, and not give up when things get uncomfortable.

After I'd befriended my grief I realised I needed an outlet for the helplessness. The only control I had was over myself.

And so I decided to embrace the discomfort and to make it a friend: I registered for the Ironman 70.3. I saw no reason not to manifest the psychic pain in a physical way.

Your body has to be conditioned to be trained.

I had to learn to re-establish and recalibrate my relationship with pain. To understand that it is okay to feel, to be aware. It's okay to have discomfort, to be restless and frustrated. The strain, the twinges, the aches I experienced during training reminded me that I was chasing something I wanted in the long term even if, in the short term, things weren't always easy or comfortable.

In fact, running hills or waking up at five in the morning was difficult. Then, a few weeks before the race I started to feel confident, fit and amazing. I'd become comfortable with putting myself through various degrees of agony. Something had shifted.

Soon, I was faced with something called the double brick

during training: a 40 km cycle followed by a 5 km run, twice in quick succession. I became excited to see how I'd handle it and whether I could pace myself.

I used to be really scared of these things. Running felt like an obligation because it was good for me. But during this training, I grasped that from enforced discomfort came growth. It was a revelation to me. It gave me a new sense of my own agency. With Ironman 70.3, you have nowhere to hide. Nobody's helping you through that swim. Nobody's helping you through that half-marathon. Nobody's helping you through that 90 km cycle. Nobody.

IT'S JUST YOU

I had broken out of the tyranny of my own comfort.

Mastery is wonderful. It provides a new ease, a new confidence, but it can also become its own dead zone. It's you on autopilot. It's you breezing through. It's you wearing your ease like a T-shirt that has become discoloured and shapeless while you cruise blithely by.

Sometimes you need a sister to call attention to your creeping sloppiness, or a setback to remind you that past successes don't guarantee future ones. Or a lockdown to throw your complacency into stark relief.

In July 2021, fifteen months after COVID-19 struck, I

accomplished the Half Ironman and placed sixth in my age group. I was elated. On every Zoom call I was dangling my medal in front of my computer screen and I revelled in the congratulations, even though what counted was how I felt about myself, not how others reacted to my joy.

External manifestations of success are great for self-esteem, and it really was fantastic to reach a peak point of physical fitness. Pushing yourself beyond what you think you're mentally, physically and psychologically capable of peels away the layers you've created to help yourself avoid anguish. Under all of those piles of comfort, the real you waits to welcome you to parts of yourself you didn't know existed.

I find the same is necessary for finding quiet and space in life. It too requires fitness and practice.

Just recently, I was speaking to a woman who is in very good shape. She takes physical fitness very seriously – but works only on her physical being. In conversation, she asked a few things about me and my life, and I told her that I make space to look after every aspect of my health every day of my life. I run or walk or work out. I care about what I put into my body. And I work on my soul.

I visit shamans and gurus, for instance, whose wisdom and insights teach me how much I have to learn. Recently, I visited a healer who told me that she works with paedophiles. I was shocked. Then she told me that if I believed in empathy,

I had to believe in empathy for *all* people. That includes paedophiles. No one wants to talk to them or listen to them or help them. They are ostracised from society. But this woman allows herself to have empathy – love, in fact, the way that religions teach it – with all people. How, she asked me, would they ever be able to fix their lives if no one ever listened to them or engaged with them? It taught me that we all judge others, and that we feel empowered by that judgement. In other words, the only thing that my judgement of others is good for is making me feel better about myself. That is narrow and weak, and I now know that I need to try harder at being empathetic, if I value empathy as a principle.

So, I work on myself. I meditate, take time to think and, in recent months, I have been dedicated to family constellations, a form of therapy that draws on our understandings of family, and how past pain we may not even be conscious of can influence our lives. I have recently become interested in the teachings of Joe Dispenza called Blessing of the Energy Centres.

I have always been interested in understanding myself. I seek out learning and growth. In some way, I feel like I should have had the physical, financial, and most importantly, the psychological tools to manage the crisis that was thrust on all of us in 2020. And yet, I struggled. The largeness of the loss felt overwhelming. The anguish was all-consuming.

But I faced down the inner demons that emerged when the outer demons took hold and I started to feel ready to face forward. Life ahead, though, felt unknowable. The next thing I had to face was the abnormal.

ORMAL

ABNO

ABNORM

A

RMAL

PART 2: ABNORMAL

FACE FORWARD

If the anguish I experienced could be described as a posture, it would be of a person with their shoulders slumped and their eyes on the ground. But I had come through that. I had pulled my shoulders back slowly, turned my face up gradually. I had honoured my sadness and slowly my anxiety started to ease and I could look up at the world around me again. I had come out of myself, and back into the world.

The world is a changed place, though.

WHEN THE OLD WAYS DIE TO MAKE WAY FOR THE NEW

Have you heard of technological singularity? It is a theoretical time somewhere in the future when technological growth goes into a self-perpetuating sort of growth, when it leaves human control and becomes irreversible. Technology, one hypothesis says, according to Wikipedia, will enter into a 'runaway reaction' of self-improvement cycles, each new and more intelligent generation appearing more quickly, causing 'an intelligence explosion' that will result in a powerful super-intelligence that surpasses all human intelligence.

This is the artificial intelligence (AI) future we have heard or read about, the one that provokes mostly fear and trepidation. Current predictions are that the singularity will arrive in 2029.

That's not far away.

Technology, however, is thought to be neutral. Whose hands it is in – that is the scarier part. Governments will use it in a way that serves them. In some Scandinavian countries we have blockchain democracies, while others are turning into digital dictatorships.

For many, many people, the singularity sounds too improbable to be real. It is written off as a fantasy, the stuff of sci-fi novels and blockbuster movies. And if it is given any credit at all, many people simply shy away from considering it fully because it seems unfathomable. How do we think about things we cannot imagine? It seems like an impossible paradox.

If someone predicted, at the turn of this century, that people would hijack planes to fly them into the World Trade Centre, or that a virus would enforce worldwide quarantine, plunging economies into crisis, you'd probably have put it down to doom-mongering or false prophecy.

Use that same lens to consider AI. It might seem improbable or even preposterous to you now, but let's take it from the many thousands of people who work in the philosophy and realities of tech: the outlook is clear. Tech is going to start recreating itself and we humans, who have believed ourselves top of the pile for so many decades, might have to admit that we are no longer the kingpins of the universe.

I used to see myself as an optimist. I believed that with

the right attitude, everything was just peachy. But when you believe it's all glaring sunshine, you might not notice the many shadows that so much optimism can create. Then one day I read about the concept of being a 'possibilist'. A possibilist looks for opportunity, regardless of whether the circumstances seem right or wrong, sunny or cloudy. Possibilism feels to me like a maturing of optimism and I align myself now with that definition.

We have gone through a lot, but neither radiant optimism nor gloomy pessimism are helpful attitudes. Both become ends in themselves and shut down our options.

In the spirit of possibilism, let us take a direct look at what the future might hold, so that we can see what is required of us in this next phase of our individual and social progress.

THE SAECULUM

In their 1997 book *The Fourth Turning*, Neil Howe and William Strauss describe a concept called the saeculum, an ancient unit of time that spans roughly eighty to a hundred years. The idea is that the cycle of human experience approximates the length of a human life.

Together, the four turnings of the saeculum comprise history's seasonal rhythm of growth, maturation, entropy, and destruction.

The First Turning is a high, an upbeat era of strengthening institutions and weakening individualism. It is peaceful living at its best. In living memory, that would be between 1946 and 1964 when the United Nations and the International Monetary Fund, space programmes, TVs and jets all came into being.

The Second Turning is an awakening, a passionate era of spiritual upheaval, when the civic order comes under attack from a new values regime. It's when individuals will have strong opinions about where their allegiance lies. From 1964 to 1984, Woodstock, computers and the *Star Wars* trilogy entered our worlds.

The Third Turning is an unravelling, a downcast era of strengthening individualism and weakening institutions, when the old civic order decays and the new values regime implants, providing what could be called a fragile peace at best. From 1984 to 2008, this era – according to Howe and Strauss – was marked by disintegration of society, the fall of the Berlin Wall, the Tiananmen Square riots in China, the rise and expansion of the feminism movement, the *Exxon Valdez* oil spill and the 9/11 attacks.

The Fourth Turning, the one which has presented itself now, is a crisis, a clear-cut era of secular upheaval, when values shift and the old civic order is replaced with a new one. This smudges out what came before and creates a vacuous uncertainty. From 2008 to 2028 we'll be gripped by financial crises, massive job losses, war – against visible and invisible enemies – and political divisions.

This Fourth Turning becomes relevant to us by creating a context for our current state of chaos. Based on the analysis of historical patterns, this decade appears to be the climax of the Fourth Turning, marking the beginning of the end. Indeed, Russia's invasion of Ukraine on 24 February 2022 was an event whose magnitude was to be expected of our current time. At the time of writing, the invasion was just twenty-one days old, making it too early to speculate about how the invasion would end and just how far its devastating effects would reach. But already its ramifications for the global economy, foreign policy and rearmament in Europe, power relations between east and west, our reliance on fossil fuels and even, potentially, food security appear to be seismic.

Putin's war – fuelled in part by a fight for an old world order, a desire to return his country's borders to how they were in imperial times – marks a crescendo of the vestiges of 'old men' energy. It's the energy of a generation raised in the scarcity mindset brought about by World War II, and it's evoking in many the spectre of World War III. It's something of a crisis of consciousness, too, these actions of a generation that seems unaware of what it is doing. What's needed is for those who think like Putin, whose grief for what is past manifests as anger as they've never been taught to process their grief, to develop the courage to move aside and open the way for the new. As Dr Caroline Leaf reminds us in her work with grief, quoting CS Lewis: 'I sat with my anger long enough until she told me her real name was grief.'

THE SAECULUM AND WESTERN CULTURE

The notion of the saeculum, or even the idea of cycle, is uncomfortable for a modern western culture that prefers linearity and a sense of progression rather than circularity. Both the leadership and public in the western world were unprepared for the scale of the pandemic and its effects. Linear thinking, according to American political scientist Francis Fukuyama, signalled the end of human sociocultural evolution, through the western thinking that economic growth is an inalienable right and policymakers should pursue whatever it takes to keep it going.

This is capitalism at its worst: the idea that we should do whatever we can to keep linear growth going, we should always be in harvest mode, which is causing havoc in our lives and to all life on earth. It's a broken model. The idea of circularity is much more in tune with the planet's natural rhythms and movement through the seasons.

THE FOURTH TURNING AND CHANGE

We are deep into the Fourth Turning and it's changing how we feel about ourselves, our culture, our nations, our future, as uncertainty shakes the economy, politics and our realities. This new era involves Gen Zs and Boomers fighting over the shape of the world as it is and as it is to become, as one generation enters old age and another enters young adulthood, which happens every eighty years or so according to Howe and Strauss's theory. Teen climate activist Greta Thunberg sparring with US president Donald Trump on social media is probably the most visible symbol of that.

'JUST IN TIME' VERSUS 'JUST IN CASE'

The Fourth Turning is the end of the *complicated* world, and the next turning will usher in the start of the *complex* world. The complicated world has business models geared towards repeated patterns, using mathematics and accounting, with eventual automation, developing high levels of efficiency. They work on economies of scale and they are a cancer.

A *complex* world, by comparison, has patterns, but they don't repeat themselves. It cannot be predicted, making it uncertain. It requires complex technology, not yet developed, to automate. Economies of scale and efficiency were key in the complicated world – a 'just in time' mentality. In the complex world, we need economies of learning and robustness – a 'just in case' approach, a response to our inability to predict what lies ahead.

Most people are well-rehearsed in responding to complicated world rules. Ironically, the more educated a person is, the less likely it is they'll see a solution when it is not within the framework in which they were taught to think. Their expertise could be the stumbling block in understanding the new world, which requires sharpness and quickness. Intellectual collateral will, as the future unfolds, be drawn more from disruptive, rather than innovative, behaviour. And intuition will be prized over intelligence.

As we evolve from the Fourth to the First Turning, there are assumptions and biases – about ourselves, our business models, and our clients and customers – that require reframing.

1. The confirmation bias: Are we going with what we know when we have doubts about how to proceed, or are we exploring unique approaches?
2. The optimism bias: Are we feeling it's so good it can't possibly fail, without taking the changing context or business environment into account? Can we become possibilists instead?
3. The status quo bias: When we believe change is bad for business.
4. The doom bias: Are we paralysed into doing nothing

because all the scenarios look daunting? Being constantly on our phones can hook us into manufactured drama. Can we unhitch ourselves from developing a bias towards bleakness?

5. 'Short-termism': Is this western model of addiction to short-term cycles of quarterly profits as a measurement tool working for us, our employees and our businesses? Are we diluting our responsibility by refusing to acknowledge the effect our decisions are having on others because we're deliberately removed or because our choice offers convenience?

6. Milking the plant: Are we leaving anything else on the table for those who come after us? The boardroom might make a decision to reach a target that has to be implemented by others, no matter what. Decisions like this might leave the plant broken, the employees stressed to the point of illness, resources used up and the product defunct.

7. Decolonising the future: When England, Holland, France, Spain, Portugal and Belgium colonised the world, they stripped locals in the countries they grabbed of their rights and their children's rights for decades into the future, and the whole world is still smarting from the consequences. Are we making conscious decisions that will benefit all people into the future, so that the

generations that follow us will not be left with nothing? How are we colonising – or decolonising – the future?

So, the question is, what do we do with this knowledge and how do we change our trajectory to one of progress, when we are currently idling?

In a small municipality in Japan, they divided the council into people working on current issues, and people working on looking ten to fifteen years ahead. Eventually, the whole council started working on the future plans for the town. Once we can see it and mobilise it, it's the best way to work: with the future in mind.

Awareness is the key to everything. Become aware of your biases and blind spots, and you can see the future more clearly.

THE HERO'S JOURNEY

Based on the saeculum scenario, the pandemic or something similar could have been predicted and, based on this, we have an idea of how future scenarios might unfold. Once we have scrutinised our assumptions and biases, let's look at how we, as business leaders and entrepreneurs, can prepare for the next cycle.

- The first thing to acknowledge is that, while we do not have any control over what happens, we do have control over how we *respond*. Because we are now aware of endings, we better understand what living in the present means. We are now all embarking on what is commonly known as 'the hero's journey'.

- Secondly, we need to acknowledge that, by transitioning from sadness for what was or could have been to accepting the abnormal and unknown, we're letting go of everything that no longer serves us. Relying on our past success as a business could be the prison that prevents us from accessing liberating ideas and innovative ways of tackling our future business model.

In mythology and storytelling through the ages, there has been the idea of 'the hero's journey', in which someone embarks on a new venture, either of their own choosing or because they have been forced to in some way. Their quest is often full of surprises and trials. There is a major crisis somewhere along the way, but the hero triumphs over it and comes home transformed.

The hero's journey is an adventure, and having the courage to explore untrodden paths is reason for celebration. It requires recovery and response through reinvention and reimagination. Reimagining gives us the space to say goodbye to the past and to project an image onto the world we choose to live in.

Stop with me for a second and offer yourself the gift of time to imagine yourself in an unfathomable new world, one which requires an entirely new skill set.

This pandemic is raising the alarm for history to once again stir. The bubonic plague, the Spanish flu and now COVID-19 are the clarion calls for change. In other words, it's likely globalisation will end, immigration restrictions will multiply and isolationism will return. Industrial policy will be back. In fact, Neil Howe asserts that one absolute rule of history is that crisis eras are marked by large, dictatorial, authoritarian and intrusive regimes. The good news is that the cycle following this one is one of growth.

So, as the world around us crumbles, we should be asking ourselves how to prepare for the spring. What can we cast aside as no longer necessary, and what should we now take on board to prepare us for the way ahead?

THE FUTURE OF LEADERSHIP

One of the most shocking aspects of the rise of COVID-19 was the sudden increase in extremely strict border control. There was also a very strong *need* to control. Governments and politicians lean heavily into this totalitarian kind of rule, telling their citizens what they can and cannot do.

Our freedoms had to be restricted to some degree, especially when no one really understood what they were dealing with, but our resistance has been great. The question was, how would politicians ease these controls? Or would they continue to enforce them, because of the power it gave them?

Let's go back to the Baby Boomers and the countries not led by them – New Zealand, Finland, Sweden, all led by decisive women in their thirties and forties. Countries that are not working are generally led by old men.

A rolling kind of citizens' revolt is under way, popping into wider public consciousness in various places, questioning systems that have been entrenched for a long time. The first time we really saw the ability of social media and the internet to empower people was during the Arab Spring of the early 2010s. The movement brought about a groundswell of people refusing to accept authority. GameStop, #MeToo and Black Lives Matter were all examples of the collapse of the authority of white- and male-dominated ideas of how the world should work, and they all gained momentum through questioning and collaborative connection over the internet. Power not for the few but for the many.

But no one gives up power without a fight. The Republicans tried to hold on, sending Donald Trump – possibly the worst version of Republican thinking – to play on the international stage. (As a side note, I have realised that perhaps Donald Trump was my first lesson in extending empathy to all people, as the medicine woman tried to show me recently. I don't want to get into politics, but Trump was such an easy target to despise on so many levels. The longer he stayed in office, the more I saw him as nothing more than a hurt eight-year-old boy so that, even while he caused mayhem, I felt sorry for the mess of a human he actually is.) Brexit was another a clear sign of the old wanting to hold on to power, and it cost the United Kingdom billions.

As world events like Russia's invasion of Ukraine – and the tension between China and Taiwan – are revealing, leadership is collapsing and creating in its wake a massive levelling. There is a heavy inertia. We need new Mandelas and new Gandhis to remind us about the better side of our nature, because the tendency for retributive tribalism is so powerful. It is critical that someone takes the high road. The possibilities that exist need to be stitched together; we – ordinary people – need to meet in the middle, instead of just waiting for our generals to fill in the gap.

'Barn's burned down – / now / I can see the moon' is a poem by Mizuta Masahide, a seventeenth-century Japanese poet and samurai. What can we see beyond the ruins of our broken world?

Something has ended. We need courage as we pass from this winter of destruction into a spring of opportunity. And we can only do this by transforming ourselves and extending the value of that to situations and people around us. *We* need to lead, by showing that vulnerability is not weakness, that we can change, adapt and reinvent. That, while we value and celebrate intelligence, we must not do so at the expense of our intuition.

As we begin to do that, here are the questions you need to ask yourself:

- Do you have a support system of people who can keep you grounded? I have friends who keep me humble, challenge me and support me.
- Do you have an executive coach, a mentor or a confidant? I believe in accessing other people's wisdom and expertise. I have tutors, coaches and healers for the things I cannot learn on my own.
- How have you responded to criticism in the past? Do you think that your way's the best way and you'll brook no argument? Might you be able to find ways to hear criticism without experiencing anger, and use that feedback to make things better?
- What feedback have you received about not walking the talk?
- Do you overtly demand special treatment, or perhaps demand it without even realising it? On what do you base your idea of your specialness? I think, for instance, about that man on the plane I saw who engaged in a friendly way with someone who looked like him, but hardened at

the sight of someone who did not look like him. What, I wonder, did he think made the white man – a mirror of himself – special enough to deserve his friendliness?
- Do you invite others into the spotlight?
- Do you isolate yourself in your decision-making process, and do your decisions reflect what you truly value?
- Do you admit to your mistakes?
- Are you the same person at home, at work and in the spotlight?
- Do you tell yourself there are exceptions or different rules for people like you? Why?

These are some of the questions I asked myself to create some anchor points in the strangeness around me. It helped me adjust to transition and to begin to imagine different futures.

Resilience – advancing despite adversity

Entrepreneurial leadership requires embracing change and a new way of doing things, but the default button for many leaders has been to hone in on being resilient. What they believe resilience to be is powering through and keeping on going, just to make it over the next hurdle. Just keep talking and make sure communication is on track, they say, and we'll get through this.

But perhaps this has added to the confusion by using old remedies to solve new or evolving problems.

Firstly, resilience is only important if you've focused it in the right direction. If you focus it in the wrong direction, it becomes pointless. Brian Chesky, CEO of Airbnb, used an analogy that really stuck a chord with me – if you're in a house that's being renovated and one side suddenly starts burning, you need to understand that just putting the fire out is not going to get you to where you need to go. Likewise, just focusing on the renovations and not putting the fire out will most likely burn the whole house down.

I find it's been hugely beneficial to focus on one or the other, but not on both. Trying to put out a fire while we're doing the renovations is not just frantic and stressful, it's ultimately unhelpful. Neither will be done effectively.

Economies of scale versus economies of learning

In the spotlight in this unfamiliar world of business that lies ahead of us is a need for new principles and fresh philosophical ideas. Driving economies of scale in a dynamic, fast-changing world is dangerous. You could find yourself in a hyper-efficient business that is facing the wrong direction.

What we require now are economies of learning. Our propulsive power lies in how quickly we can unlearn in order to relearn. It's about how quickly we pre-empt what our customers want, using data and machine learning. It's less about efficiency and more about robustness. It's about how many partners and collaborating teams you have around you, offering as many different services and products within your field.

Here today, there tomorrow

Steve Jobs set up today and tomorrow teams. When he returned to Apple, there was the Lisa computer. He despised it, but realised that he couldn't create a new computer inside Apple headquarters. He took his top engineers and a few new ones to an office away from Apple, festooned it with a pirate flag, and that was where the Macintosh that usurped the Lisa was born. In other words, he created a tomorrow team – with its spyglass trained on what was ahead – to upend the today team that was keeping the ship steady.

New roles for today's leaders

MIT recently released an article suggesting that there are four roles today's leaders should fulfil:

1. The Conductor: Coordinates the efforts of virtual teams.
2. The Catalyst: Sparks innovation and collaboration for in-person meetings. Brings out the best in people.
3. The Coach: Balances empathy with pushing people out of their comfort zones.
4. The Champion: Advocates for their team and finding ways to position them for success.

I suggest another role: the Captain.

The Captain is the business of you. You are a brand, and your skills can be monetised. You can develop a direct relationship with the people you serve and who serve you.

'You do you' is a saying that has become very popular, but when you unpick the cliché, it's all there: you are your own brand of uniqueness, authenticity and robust individual expression. And no one can stand in for that or do you better than you can. If previous iterations of our world required us to blend in, to form part of a pattern that was accepted as the 'correct' one, the only one, the future world demands individuality. This is daunting and it might make you feel like it is exposing, but it's also exhilarating.

So: who are *you*? And what is it about your brand, your market and what you're selling that makes it – and you – unique?

Here is how personal brand is playing out on social media, for instance: individual footballers have, in some cases, more followers than the popular football clubs they belong to.

Having started out as a young entrepreneur and then evolved down different paths, this is how I've learnt to adjust and respond to this complex world: I invested more, re-invented harder, learnt to be more patient and engaged with people with skill sets different from my own. My goal was to prepare on every front while we move through this phase of uncertainty. In this time of crisis and transformation, I overcommunicate with the people I collaborate with, moving with deliberation from transactional to transformational leadership styles and shifting from a digital focus to a more virtual one. What I mean by this is that the digital world in which we currently mostly operate is a static one, whereas the virtual world is more direct and 'live'. One way to think of this is the rise of TikTok, which is fast outstripping Instagram.

A few years ago, not long before COVID hit, I decided to start the Future Self Academy with a friend of mine. It would provide training based on my books and talks and teachings. We both invested money. With every business I start, I have a victory condition and a failure condition. Building these in beforehand protects me from banging my head against a brick wall when the going gets tough. COVID arrived and my failure condition followed. We collapsed what we had started, realising also that this was the wrong direction to take, because digital is static and everything is moving towards live now.

Understanding that this phase is seasonal should bring you the calm to be creative and entrepreneurial. As old structures fall away, there's a unique opportunity for reinvention; with that, the journey towards future scenarios becomes one of adventure. And could turn you into a hero in more ways than just as the lead in your own story.

THE FUTURE OF OUR ECONOMIES

To really understand COVID-19 and climate change, we should take a look at the core of these afflictions, which are socially, not environmentally, driven. If we take out superfluous economic activity – that is, if we make less – we emit fewer gases and use less energy. The same applies to COVID-19. If we reduce contact, the spread of the virus is reduced and it's easier to track the infection rate.

Economies in crisis

Lockdown placed phenomenal pressure on the global economy, with many leaders calling for an easing of measures. How economies crash is quite straightforward. Traditionally, businesses exist to make a profit. If they can't produce, they can't sell. That means no profits, which means lowered employment rates. As more people lose their jobs, or fear losing their jobs, they buy less. The cycle starts again ... and we spiral into economic depression.

In a normal crisis, the remedy is simple. The government spends until we buy and work again. But that hasn't been working all that well in the past year because we didn't want the economy to recover immediately. We were encouraged not to go to work and not to spend.

After other historical crises like wars, for example, there would be a massive upscale in production. What our future may require is a system capable of reining in production that doesn't mean a loss of income. At its heart, the economy is how we use resources and turn them into *things we need to live*. Looked at this way, we start to see more opportunities for living differently that allow us to produce less without increasing suffering.

So how do we yield less in a more humane way? There have been suggestions about changing the length of the work week or giving us the option to work more slowly and under less pressure. What's required is a way to reduce our dependence on a salary to live.

'Exchange value' is when money is exchanged to drive an economy. What COVID-19 has shown is how false our belief in markets is. What has been thrown into stark relief is how critical systems are burdened, principally supply chains, social care and, critically, healthcare. These are systems that don't yield profit. People are a big cost factor and productivity growth tends to be lower than in the rest of the economy, so these systems become costlier more quickly.

These critical services are also not as highly valued as they should be. Many of the best-paid jobs exist to facilitate exchanges, but they don't serve much of a broader purpose to society. They are what anthropologist David Graeber calls 'bullshit jobs'. Yet because they make lots of money, we have lots of consultants, a huge advertising industry and a massive financial sector. Meanwhile, we have a crisis in health and social care, where people are often forced out of jobs that serve humanity and which they are called to do and get meaning from, because what they do doesn't pay them enough to live on.

Surplus jobs

The fact that so many people work in 'worthless' jobs is partly why our response to the pandemic was so poor. The pandemic forced us to recognise that many jobs are not essential, yet we lack sufficient crucial workers to respond when things go bad.

There is a veering away from the belief that we have to work to earn an income, and a transition to the idea that we deserve to live even if we cannot work. In Denmark and the UK, people were paid not to go to work, and the pandemic has reinvigorated discussions about universal basic incomes.

Public systems have come under increasing pressure to marketise and to be run as though they were businesses that have to make money. COVID-19 appears to be reversing the trend of the past 40 years of taking healthcare and labour goods out of the market and putting them into the hands of the state. States produce for many reasons, not all of them good. But unlike markets, they do not have to produce for exchange value alone. With the right intention, they give us a chance to place lives before profit.

Looking at markets in a different light

Politicians and their advisers have struggled to see worthwhile alternatives over the past 40 years. Current mindsets are underpinned by two beliefs:

- The markets are what deliver a good quality of life, so they must be protected.
- The market will always return to normal after short periods of crisis.

As governments and citizens took steps that months ago looked impossible, our ideas about how the world works changed dramatically. Now, according to economic researcher Simon Mair, there are four possible market scenarios:

- **A descent into anarchy:** This is the bleakest scenario. It's the future if we continue to rely on exchange value as our guiding principle and refuse to extend support to those who get locked out of markets by illness or unemployment. Businesses fail and workers starve because there are no mechanisms in place to protect them from harsh realities. Hospitals are not supported by extraordinary measures, and so become overwhelmed. People die. It could trigger political and social unrest, leading to a failed state and the collapse of both state and community welfare systems.
- **A robust state capitalism:** This is the dominant response

we see around the world right now. The state capitalist continues to pursue exchange value as the guiding light of the economy, but recognises that markets in crises require support from the state. The state steps in with extended welfare because workers are ill or fear for their lives. UK. Spain. Denmark.

- A radical state socialism: This is a cultural shift that places a different value at the heart of the economy. This is the future we arrive at with an extension of the measures we see in the UK, Spain and Denmark. The key here is that measures like nationalisation of hospitals, and payments to workers are seen as tools to protect markets and life itself. The state steps in to protect the parts of the economy that are essential to life: production of food, energy and shelter. Supermarket workers, delivery drivers, warehouse stackers, nurses, teachers and doctors.
- Transformation into a big society built on mutual aid: This is when we adopt the protection of life as the guiding principle of our economy. In this scenario, the state does not take a defining role. Rather, individuals and small groups begin to organise support and care within their communities. The risk is that small groups are unable to rapidly mobilise the kind of resources needed to increase healthcare capacity effectively. But it could build community support networks that protect the vulnerable.

What is clear is that all these scenarios offer reasons for fear, but also for hope. The upside is that we build a more humane system that leaves us more resilient in the face of future pandemics and other impending crises like climate change.

THE FUTURE OF TECHNOLOGY

Technological innovations and breakthroughs have brought us closer together, even at a time when many of us are social distancing. We now live and work in a hyper-connected world where geographical boundaries are blurred. It's easier than ever to bring people together, collaborate and form communities to bring about positive change. Even a single small action can make a major impact, allowing us all to play our part in building a more inclusive and caring future.

Technologically, the twenty-year jump from 2020 to 2040 will be huge. During this time, some elements of our world will change beyond recognition while others will stay reassuringly – or disappointingly – familiar. Consider the two decades leading up to 2021. Back in 1995, we were in the early days of the internet, we worked in cubicles and our computers were chunky and powered by Windows 95. There were no touch-screen phones or flat-screen TVs; people laughed at the idea of reading electronic books, and watching a home movie meant loading a clunky cassette into your VCR.

So, what will our world really be like in 2035? What does the future hold for the food we eat, the technology we use and the homes we live in? It would be tempting to roll out the clichés – food pills, flying cars and bases on the moon – but the reality will probably be less exciting. The world in 2035 will probably be much like it is today, but it will be smarter and more automated. Some innovations we might not notice, while others will knock us sideways, changing our lives forever.

Technology will change our relationship with food, health, relationships and work. We're heading into a future where improved battery technology will likely enable better electric cars, personal flying machines, hyperloop transportation systems, private space tourism and drone delivery services. We are likely to have virtual assistants (the next generation of Google Now, Siri and Cortana) to help us manage a flood of data and make sense of it.

Some of this might happen. Or none of it. Three things, however, are certain: technology will get smaller, smarter and cheaper. In fact, it will most likely get so small, smart and cheap that we'll be able to put computers and sensors into almost anything – bins will tell the council when they're full, 4K televisions will notice when we've stopped watching and turn themselves off to save power.

We're on the road to the Internet of Things, where everything is connected – not only to the internet, but also to one another. In 1883, Lord Kelvin, president of Britain's Royal Society, declared that 'X-rays will prove to be a hoax'. Arthur Summerfield, the US Postmaster General in 1959, predicted that mail would be 'delivered within hours from New York to Australia by guided missiles'. And we should be glad that Alex Lewyt's 1955 notion of 'nuclear-powered vacuum cleaners' never made it to the drawing board!

Artificial intelligence

There's been much said about artificial intelligence (AI) and unfortunately most people are afraid of it because of the bad rap it's received.

I was recently on a Mo Gawdat podcast. He's best known for writing a book called *Solve for Happy: Engineer Your Path to Joy*. He used to work for Google in the AI department, and started to realise that AI is just learning our behaviour online and then repeating it. We've misunderstood this to mean that AI is developing a level of racism or a level of bigotry or toxic masculinity, but all it's doing is copying what it's computing online. It's true that many aspects of being online are toxic, but it is only reflecting back at us. Mo says in his book that the only way for us to really start to make AI a positive addition to our lives, in the long term, is for us to be happy and to engage in a more respectful, calm and loving way. So, AI is just like the surgeon's knife: it can save you or kill you. We have a responsibility to do our part in helping to maximise its power in a way that is best for humankind.

You may not know it, but everything, and I mean *everything*, is being automated. As we speak, a revolution of consumerism is turning and a generation of apathetic consumers, making price-driven purchasing decisions, is passing. Automation is on the rise across all industries. Machine learning and engineering developments are rendering many aspects of professions obsolete.

Automation will, in my opinion, take care of every basic standard of career and business. This means that, whatever you do, there'll be a level of efficiency, recognition and pattern repetition that can be commoditised, whether you're a lawyer, doctor, writer or speaker.

Value in our world used to come from doing rudimentary things like reading and writing contracts or taking temperatures or setting bones. Now machines can do this all … and better.

The rise of the passion economy

Jeremy Rifkin, a global economist who advises China, Germany and the European Union on the Third Industrial Revolution, speaks in his book *The Zero Marginal Cost Society* about how every time something is digitised, it's repeated almost for free. The whole world is moving in this direction.

In other words, eventually just about everything will be free – think communication and photos as an example. According to Rifkin, energy and transportation are next. I'm still struggling to get my mind around that. It doesn't seem possible, but I remind myself that we would never have been able to imagine how communication and photos would ever become almost free.

Now picture this world in which everything is essentially free: how do we determine value, and on what do we place value? The only thing that isn't commodifiable and automatable yet is social and emotional connection.

What you see now is the passion economy. It's about finding and developing something you really love and profiting from it. This passion economy places a premium on softer skills such as personality and creativity. The way the passion economy empowers the individual will change our pre-existing notions of careers, putting an end to the conventional path to university, internship or climbing the corporate ladder.

By developing new products or services that are cheaper, simpler and more convenient, workers in the passion economy can tap into large segments of the economy which they could not previously access or afford to enter. In this way, the passion economy business has the potential to disrupt the structure of big businesses.

The passion economy reflects the world we had before the

Industrial Revolution, when there were small towns and villages dotted around, but very few big cities. Urbanisation, along with the increase in the world's population, was the dominant demographic trend of the late twentieth century, but before that, every village had its own butcher, baker and candlestick maker. These were run by families who had passed skills and craftsmanship down through generations. While not every member of the family might have been passionate about their required involvement, the business was built on personal knowledge and pride in a noble occupation that delivered necessary services and products for life to continue within the community. They might have been able to service the people within their own village, and perhaps a village or two beyond their own, but transportation wasn't as efficient as it is today.

Now, the creator or passion economy is more likely to be run by the individual rather than an entire family – though that is not excluded at all – and, because of technology and the borderless world we live in, we can service anyone anywhere in the world. With five billion people on the internet – and with predictions saying this will soon increase by 50 per cent – all you really have to do is get 0.000001 per cent to pay you $2 a month and you're going to be living large for generations to come.

So, it's important for us to understand the new dynamics of business and to uphold and apply ourselves to this new way of expanding and reaching millions of people from the comfort of our homes.

At the time of writing, the passion economy was worth $38 billion. It has been growing steadily since 2010, with double-digit growth especially since the Great Resignation of 2021, when workers quit their jobs at historic rates – leading to the (as yet unnamed) Great Reignition of the Entrepreneur.

The passion economy as a disruptor

Disruption, a theory developed by Harvard Business School professor Clayton Christensen in the 1990s, is a concept that has been widely referenced but is largely misunderstood. Contrary to popular belief, disruptive innovations are not breakthrough innovations that make good products better. Instead, they are innovations that either enter at the bottom of the market and serve a lower-profit segment, or that target consumers who previously could not access or afford a product or service. This process is enabled by technological change and business model innovations. Because disruptive innovations tend to be seen initially as inferior to existing solutions, they're often underrated by market entrants who tend to focus on serving large existing markets with greater profitability.

Engineer, physician and entrepreneur Peter Diamandis explains that disruptive ideas usually conform to the Six Ds. They are digitised, deceptive, disruptive, dematerialised (think for instance of the printed photograph versus the digital picture), demonetised and democratised; in short, 'A chain reaction of technological progression, a road map of rapid development that always leads to enormous upheaval and opportunity.'

What is required of us is to hone our interests, rather than to learn skills that we believe look good in the eyes of our employers or parents or spouses. By doing so, we move power out of big institutions and into the hands of individuals, placing emphasis on entrepreneurship, creativity, speciality and accountability.

The passion economy is not just about being your own boss; it's about offering unique content and engaging communities. Technology plays the role of the enabler, not the intermediary. You can now share your passion on a paying platform, which goes beyond social media and is more tailored towards creators' needs. In fact, the more we hear how social media is playing with our minds and wasting our time, the more advantageous it becomes to use these platforms.

New tools make it easier than ever for prospective workers to earn an income by tapping into passions and unique skills. Examples include writers on Substack publishing their own subscription newsletters, professional video game streamers on Twitch and Caffeine, video course creators on Teachable and Podia, and online teachers on K-12 learning platforms Outschool and Juni Learning.

But what if you don't have any hobbies, don't know what your passion is … and hate your job? I have a simple piece of advice for you. I found that following my curiosity, instead of worrying about what my passion might be, was an easier way for me to connect with what I wanted to do. Curiosity is a gateway to passion. Passion doesn't just arrive because we're looking for it – we've got to follow the golden thread of what interests us.

You will come to realise in the process that you are curious in a unique way. No one can be as inquisitive about a particular thing, from your particular angle, as you can.

Once a combination and range of curiosities come together, we will have developed a passion. You – and only you – hold the potential to offer that passion as a service to your community or to your clients.

I have written previously about how educational institutions have trained thousands of people to be the same. It's caused a surplus of very smart people, educated in more or less the same ways. The passion economy provides an escape route out of sameness, a road towards personal fulfilment and a chance to provide singular, exceptional contributions to the world at large.

We will be aided in our unique undertakings by AI, which is waiting in the wings to make the repetitive parts of our jobs less demanding on our time. In the new world we are entering,

AI technologies are based on human–machine cooperation, not human displacement. By harnessing the power of that, we create time to do meaningful, fulfilling work, rather than just sitting in front of the computer for eight hours at a time.

Futurist Liselotte Lyngsø warns that it is a big mistake to think of ourselves as becoming machines in the AI future. 'We really have to find out about human nature. Empathy will be important and difficult for the machines to master ... We have to tease out human capabilities and find out how to find our individual potentials.'

Now is the time to ask yourself some hard questions:

- Are you willing to let go of the herd mentality and carve your own niche?
- Are you prepared to spend an hour a day being curious, following the golden thread of your passion, so that over time you become not just informed, but an expert?
- Are you open to an informal education? Are you able to pursue the things that ignite your excitement without expecting to get a certificate or a diploma for your efforts?

Philosophers and economists have predicted the displacement of humans by machines for a long time, but this hasn't affected the labour market the way they expected it to. The expectation was that there would be too much free time because of machines or automation. But now, all economic interactions are looking for limitless growth and sustainability. Hopefully, the next generations are more open to new systems that are not just capitalism or socialism, but which help to build on sustainability and inclusion, where legislation promotes equality and AI is designed in such a way that it truly benefits and works in communion with humankind.

Imagine a world in which AI makes your life less complicated and you are freed up to do work you like because you enjoy it, rather than work you have to do to pay the rent. In this imagined world, leisure and work could be entirely reframed.

The metaverse

In the next five years, we will all begin to spend time in the metaverse. And if that seems unlikely to you, remember that there was a time when none of us thought we'd be on Facebook, yet here we are.

The metaverse is just a combination of three things: XR, AI and blockchain (a system in which a record of transactions made in bitcoin or another cryptocurrency is maintained across several computers that are linked in a peer-to-peer network).

XR, or X-vision, is made up of AR, VR and DR. AR is augmented reality, and is when you have digitisation pushed on top of real world. So, you're still seeing the real world, but there's digitisation on top of it. VR is virtual reality. And DR is diminished reality. In the future, you'll be able to choose not to see any black dogs if you don't want to see them.

We are moving into Web 3.0 right now, and I think it is important for us to go through Web 1.0 and Web 2.0 to understand the magnitude of what's about to happen to us.

Web 1.0 started off in 1990 and went on for about fifteen years. This was the time that is referred to as the information economy. The internet was 'read only' – you could not engage with it. Web 1.0 was all about setting up infrastructure and providing access to information. Up until 2005, not all of us were on the internet.

Then Web 2.0 arrived, and it lasted from 2005 until 2020 – so it ended in that fateful year that all of us who were alive in it will always remember as the year in which everything changed. That was when we moved from the information economy to the platform economy. And in that world, you read and you write and you make small amounts of money. This is what started the creator economy. This is when we realised that we could make money by being creators online.

The biggest things that happened in this part of the Web were social media, cloud computing and smartphones. The problem with Web 2.0 is that it was centralised. Facebook, Google and Spotify just got far too big and far too powerful.

They owned all our data, they disrespected our privacy and they made all the money. We got lots of benefits, for sure, but the problems were too big to ignore.

So, welcome Web 3.0. We moved through the information economy and the platform economy and are now entering the token economy. Now we read, we write, and *we* make all the money.

Web 3.0 is used and owned by the users and builders of the internet. This forces us to think about the internet in very different ways. What made up Web 2.0 – social media, cloud computing and smartphones – is being replaced by the new pillars of Web 3.0, which are AI, blockchain and decentralisation. These three factors are now big overtones of where we are going to in the future, and this fundamentally changes the power structures in society. We are about to see a disintegration of monolithic, centralised organisations.

The best way we can see how this is happening is if you watch how many of their personal shares the CEOs of centralised Web 2.0 businesses have sold. You will get an indication that they are all selling out of Web 2.0 structures and buying into Web 3.0 structures. Amazon, Microsoft, all the big ones – their CEOs sold more shares in 2021 than they have ever done in the history of their companies.

Web 3.0 is about taking back our sovereignty online. But this puts huge pressure on us as human beings. Web 2.0 got us all to be consumers of the internet, whereas Web 3.0 forces us to become creators on the internet. This changes the dynamics of how money is made, how money is seen and how we add value to the world.

That's also why there is so much money in cryptocurrencies. It's difficult to understand, but all the money that goes into them is shared by everybody. It's not simply being sucked up by Google or Amazon. It's shared. Automatically, transparently, openly and immediately, because of blockchain and the way it works. It is a representation of a new, fair, transparent and feminine future that we're moving into.

All of this very much belongs in the section called 'abnormal'. We really do need to understand that society is about to do a flip, and if you're not willing to hurt your brain by taking in this new information you're going to get left behind.

The adventure itself – which I will address in the next section of this book – is about moving the brain away from seeking comfort in the familiar to seeking discomfort. In times of peace, it is good to be mellow and linear. In times of war, it is good to be active and dynamic.

The hypothesis is that, if we fast track to 2030 or 2040, we're going to be able to upload consciousness to computers. You'll be free to play in a multiverse. You could say *Star Trek* is finally here. With almost eight billion people on this planet, we're going to have to find solutions to take us off a trajectory of self-destruction. Instead of writing technology off, we can hatch a plan that involves recalibrating our belief systems and crafting new narratives.

THE FUTURE OF THE WORKPLACE

Humans will still be working with machines, but automation is likely to also make certain jobs redundant. Taxi drivers could be replaced with self-driving Uber cars, receptionists replaced by robots, doctors outclassed by algorithms that can plug into vast medical databases, and travel agents wiped out by trip-planning, flight-booking web services. Even writers are threatened by companies such as Narrative Science, which currently uses AI to automate the creation of sports reports and financial updates.

The flipside is that new jobs will be created: the computer engineer-slash-mechanic who fixes the self-driving Uber taxis, programmers, genome mappers and bioengineers, space tour guides, and vertical farmers. Technology will continue to shake up businesses and eliminate jobs, creating new professions we can't yet envisage.

Those of us who are employed are unlikely to continue working in traditional offices. COVID has redefined work: it's the tasks you perform, not a place you go to. Productivity is no longer measured by how long you sit at your desk for. The concepts of nine-to-five office hours and 'jobs for life' had already begun to fade into history by the time the virus arrived, and employment situations like that are likely to become increasingly rare.

Futurist Simon Raik-Allen suggests that we will see a return to more vibrant local communities as people work within walking distance of their homes. 'Rather than the office, or even the remote workspace, localised centres will emerge as the home of business – giant warehouses, which are used by employees from many different companies, spread around the globe ... Within each will be rooms filled with giant wall-sized screens allowing us to work in a fully virtual, telepresence model. Banks of 3D printers would be continually churning out products ordered by the local community,' Raik-Allen predicts in MYOB's *The Future of Business: Australia 2040* report.

Collaboration and communications

Collaboration is the main reason people may still go to an office. Lyngsø names 'feedback crisis' as one of the three main megatrends on the horizon. Because we communicate via technology all the time, we become more removed from ourselves and from others. We do not have the feedback that comes from others during real-time, face-to-face conversations – facial expression and body language feedback – and miss out on the importance of humour and the natural development of deeper relationship by being in proximity with others. This can make us inward-looking, arrogant, too assured of ourselves and, ultimately, isolated.

Ideas, conversations and projects that take an exhausting number of fixed hours over Zoom have a momentum of their own when we are all together in a room, so coming together will remain valuable. We'll want to continue experiencing the joys of direct interaction and conversation, the nuance of natural exchange, but it will be interspersed with remote conversations in different global locations.

These are predictions, of course. But one thing is certain: flexible working is no longer in dispute – the point and purpose of the office is. Moneypenny, a company providing virtual receptions and PAs to businesses across the UK, has seen a huge shift in thinking and resources around the office. A recent survey they conducted revealed that 53 per cent of UK companies have accelerated their use of tech by one year, and 22 per cent by more than five years. Changes in tech and personnel have not only happened fast, but will also fundamentally change office operations in the long term.

Companies will have new departments called Learning and Development that will focus on developing the skill set of young talent and updating older colleagues on new developments. Peter Diamandis has a reverse-mentoring programme where he pays Gen Xs to coach him in a mentorship approach from young to old, rather than the traditional form of old to young.

While flexible working may sound ideal, the reality is that this will upend the rhythm of business and will require a remodelling of the working week and year. Women reportedly want remote working more than men do. This might make the shared physical spaces male-dominated, and there is enough evidence around for us to know that the more diverse our workplaces are, the more productive and creative our teams are, and that it improves cultural awareness. This in turn has advantages for our reputations and our marketing possibilities.

Ground gained from diversity and integration workshops could be lost or become shallow in its enforcement. Younger workers may want to return to the office, but again this could cause a cultural imbalance. Managing a multigenerational team in this new, remote work environment is not going to be a picnic. Workers, like consumers, will want a combination of 'bricks and clicks'. And it's the companies that embrace this with enthusiasm and vision that will succeed in the new era of work.

Servicing the customer of the future

Throughout the world, we're seeing established and long-standing institutions under scrutiny for unethical practices or for abusing their power. Traditionally, the customer–business interaction was more about value exchange and less about establishing and retaining a long-term relationship. But, for the first time in our recent history, COVID-19 has forced corporates to shift their attention from the bottom line to retaining customers. Without a customer who trusts us, as many companies discovered, we no longer exist. As the world crashed to a halt during this phase of strangeness, leading conglomerates suddenly found themselves competing for spend from a far more digitally savvy, conscious and selective consumer, often with uncertain and restricted resources.

The consumer shift

Governed by solidarity and sharing a common human affliction, the consumer shift has been towards buying *into* what companies stand for, rather than simply buying *from* them. Brand, purpose and reputation has taken on new impetus and carried equal weight to safety, security and convenience.

During the pandemic, probably for the first time, customers have felt that companies favoured them and their employee well-being above bottom-line profit. Companies that act with empathy and compassion gain more trust, and consumers, through networks and digital access, hold more power in dictating the shape of products and services than ever before.

The trust conundrum

But here's the conundrum. How do businesses retain the trust of customers who've bought into their ethos? One thing that is becoming increasingly clear is that tried and trusted boardroom tactics no longer cut it with this new type of consumer. The dynamics of experience delivery have been challenged. The main craze a few years ago was to create experiences for our clients so that they would remember the experience for long afterwards, but then everyone started doing it. Now we're seeing a new approach, called transformation delivery, where you literally transform as a human. CrossFit and Burning Man are two examples of true transformational interaction.

We have to ditch the sales pitch and ramp up other ways of cementing trust. Public relations with authentic content can create a connection with the people we wish to serve, but this means not just churning out what we think they want. It means being sincere and real and human. What does our company care about? How can we share that through thought-leadership pieces and on discussion platforms? These are all ways to encourage our customer to reach out to us and seek advice from us. People want to connect with people, not with bots or scripts or algorithms.

Those in power are often threatened by new ideas. The trick is to sell without selling. Allow our customers to react to us when they are relaxed, going through a newspaper, watching an interview, scrolling through LinkedIn, Facebook or Instagram, or reading a magazine. When they're at ease and we're talking to them about the new wave and the new way the world markets are going, we become more of a voice of reason, a voice of the future – and that way, you shift the dynamic of being a push salesman to a position of pull. When you create a pull and your customer reaches out to you, and you're gaining their trust in that interaction. This takes longer than usual, but it's worth it in the long run.

People don't want to be sold to, they want to be advised. They don't want to be sought, they want to find the people who can help them.

Applying the same culture of compassion to the customer and the employee

The customer has become more digitally savvy, expecting effortless interactions. Customers of all ages have made behavioural changes by harnessing the internet to make their daily lives easier. They also have the tools to share their experiences across vast networks.

Since they have easier access to both information and to dissemination, and because they are more discerning in terms of the kinds of companies they want to do business with, the way you treat *all* people is going to matter for your livelihood in the future. Your customers will no longer care only about whether you're treating them well – they will care about how you treat the people who work with and for you. And since it's easy to shop around now, if you don't pass muster they'll move on to companies they perceive as doing better at being human. And they will use their social networks to say why they're doing so.

A recent KPMG report indicated that a whopping 41 per cent of customers say it's important for customers to be assured that a company's employees are treated well in their jobs. Your employees are no longer invisible to your potential clients. And if your empathy doesn't extend to your employees, co-workers and service providers, the customer is likely to feel that they have no basis for a trust relationship with you.

As bricks-and-mortar stores shift to incorporate the digital world into an extension of themselves, we enter the era of dispersive customer interaction. This means customers want an experience tailor-made to their needs. A coffee shop or photocopy shop may be on a dying trajectory but if you focus on bringing coffee to the home office or providing an online photocopy delivery service, you'll be providing dispersive flow.

While the business world is racing towards adaptive business tactics, the consumer has become empowered with networks and devices, and they're demanding better, kinder, more empathetic engagement with the world and its people.

We always run the risk of making mistakes, but if we have established a relationship with our customers by being open, transparent and authentic, they will be more forgiving and understanding should the pawpaw ever hit the fan.

That's what loyalty is. That's what relationship means.

And that's what the future of our working lives will built around.

THE FUTURE OF EDUCATION

It's always easy to make pronouncements on how things were easier back in the day, but I do often wonder whether any generation has been quite so *aware* of the uncertainty it faces as ours is.

We had predictable routes into adulthood that were governed by tradition, culture and law, and which required us to fit into certain rigid identities, ways of working and ways of fitting in. The whiter you were, the more likely you were to be in a higher-paid and more secure position. The browner you were, the more you'd have to fight. If you were a woman, you were expected to get married, want children and serve your husband. If you were male, you were expected to want a relationship with a woman, not a man, and to act as though you were that woman's intellectual superior.

If your family had a family business, you could be expected

to be employed there. If you were a farmer, you knew that winter was followed by spring and new life. If you studied and became a doctor, you knew you'd be more financially secure than any nurse could ever hope to be. If you studied structural engineering, you'd probably build bridges. If you were a bank clerk, you'd likely stay with the same bank, working your way up the ranks, until retirement. And if you were a night owl, whose energy and ideas came to them when the sun started to set, well, that was just tough, because the rest of the world wanted your best between nine and five during daylight hours.

Nothing now feels secure or predictable. The world is becoming accepting of ways of being beyond the established patterns. Questionable old practices are falling by the wayside, and the doors of opportunity are opening to more kinds of people than ever before. This is great news on so many levels, but change is always destabilising, even for those who benefit.

Plus, technological advancement – so fast most of us can't really keep up with it – makes us insecure about our future ability to earn money.

How does learning and training fit into all of this? What should we be teaching children of schoolgoing age? Is the rigid education system we currently have – one that was mostly invented in the nineteenth century and which didn't change much in the century that followed it – creating the kind of robust, resilient, flexible people the future needs?

What can we predict about our futures when, as we're often told, 90 per cent of the jobs our kids will have when they finish school haven't even been invented yet? And how are children supposed to choose their subjects?

My feeling is that the only thing we can focus on is *behaviour*. We can teach children the behaviour of adaptability and of reframing challenges as opportunities.

Hollywood has created some hellish ideas about a future with AI, convincing us that robots are going to take away our jobs. Fear fuels negativity and pessimism, but we cannot let our children lose hope. Let them take whatever subjects interest them. It's not the subjects that will define their success in the new world. It's other stuff.

What you as a parent can do is to teach them from early on to understand themselves and their passions. Allow them to play – the most powerful education of all is self-discovery, which is activated in play – and support them in their interests. Go with them where their curiosity takes them.

Show them also what interests you: the stars, horse-racing, growing tomatoes, rock climbing, whatever allows them to look around, observe, take in, take part in, move their bodies and expand their worlds. Not only will you be showing them how to nurture passion, but you'll be forming a bond and teaching them about trust, empathy and relating.

When the new world arrives – the scary one in which you

imagined your child will have no use in the workforce – you will have prepared them plenty. Let's say, for instance, that your child has studied law. It has been shown that lawyers take 90 hours to read a contract at 70 to 80 per cent accuracy. Machines can do it in 0.4 seconds, with an accuracy rate of 99 per cent. We simply cannot compete.

So, we won't.

And, if truth be told, you won't need to. Not with the robot, at any rate. You will still have to know your law and understand contracts. But your real value is the emotional and social cohesion between yourself, your client and the machine.

So, give your children the widest range of experiences you can. Don't make it a competition or a mission – make it a family adventure. Whether it's as mundane as choosing a new light fitting for the kitchen together or as mind-blowing as a once-in-a-lifetime experience of flying in a helicopter, your children will be ignited by seeing their parents engaged, excited, curious and, yes, passionate. Because how else do you align with your own curiosity and passion if you do the same thing year in and year out?

In a book called *Range: Why Generalists Triumph in a Specialized World*, David Epstein argues for us to expose ourselves to a wide range of skill sets. Real life happens, he says, where rules are multiple, goals change and there is no simple measure of progress. We live in complex environments for which our brains have been trained. Generalists – people who know about many things – are better adapted than specialists, who know everything about just one thing. Even Malcolm Gladwell – who made the 10 000-hour rule famous in his book *Outliers*, which is about exceptional people who became expert because of enormous dedication to one thing – says that he likes being taught new things.

If we think about that hypothetical lawyer of the future, what the prospective graduate should be asking themselves before they embark on an expensive university career is, 'Is law what I'm passionate about? Well, no. Actually I love gardening. I'd better start thinking about how to monetise being an avid gardener.'

The future of education is about knowing what you love so that you can find ways to make your skills, experience and knowledge sustain you. You, as parents or prospective parents, can open the doors of the world to children – not even just your own – by helping them open the door to themselves. And you do this by showing that being curious is a rewarding way to live.

The grimmest picture possible

According to TheGlobalEconomy.com data, South Africa has the dubious reputation of having the highest number of unemployed youth in the world.

Imagine heading out into the world at eighteen, or even younger, with no safety net, no mentor or mental blueprint, armed only with the knowledge that your education was less than adequate and that you're one in 7.2 million young people trying to find a job to pay rent, eat and live.

Would you be motivated?

According to the International Labour Organization, 73 million youth are unemployed globally. Six hundred million young people are expected to enter the job market in the next decade, with an estimated two hundred million job vacancies to fill.

The causes are numerous: the legacy of poor education and training, labour demand and supply mismatch, effects of global recession, slow economic growth and what is perceived as the general lack of interest in entrepreneurship.

The horror of this impossible equation dominates the headlines, but a solution is nowhere printed in black and white.

The symptoms of inertia

The status quo, then, is that there are too many school-leavers and not enough jobs. The overwhelming statistics, together with the reality of the soul-destroying, sometimes months-long sending out of CVs, applying for jobs and going for interviews, would leave even the most optimistic person a little cowed.

Inertia, in physics, is the tendency of a body to preserve its state of rest or uniform motion unless acted upon by an external force. Psychological inertia is the tendency to maintain the status quo unless you are compelled by a psychological motive to reject it.

You might argue that the young people who are on that inertia treadmill – banging out the same old steps to the same old rhythm with the same results, i.e. no job – should adjust their attitude.

But what about your own inertia? What about your organisation's inertia?

I'd say that the main reason people keep doing the same thing is because they are afraid of what they perceive to be failure, or they simply don't know how to make a change.

Taking this one step further with the premise that fear of change is what activates the brakes, we can logically conclude that the reasons for inertia do not lie with resources, time, management, or market share. Inertia can be attributed to a mindset that passes up potential opportunities because of aversion to change.

But change is exactly what this moment in history is demanding of you and of me. Being change-averse has not stopped change from finding every single one of us and hauling us out into the blinding light of the uncertain future. All around us, everything is changing. Most terrifying for many people – even those who aren't technophobic – is the rapid evolution of technology, which is enabling unimaginable things to become real.

If you're stuck in a mental rut, you're going to be unable to change quickly enough to remain immune to external forces. None of us will remain untouched, but the fleet-footed and those who bravely look change in the eye will be better equipped than those who prefer to keep things the way they have always been.

The issue with inertia, both on an individual and organisational level, is that we have essentially handed over control of our destiny. We're no longer in the driver's seat. We're waiting for the market to force change upon us. Rather than spurring change with new ideas and innovations, we've taken on a passive role.

Even if this approach has worked in the past, or is working for us now, the ease with which we're cruising along won't last forever. We'll be knocked off course at one point or another and find ourselves in one of two positions:

- The disruption may be so rapid and immense we won't be able to keep pace.
- Or we could face smaller disruptive changes that we'll be able to overcome through the status quo approach. This is dangerous because it could lull us into a false sense of security. The next time we're hit by disruption, we could be completely upended.

How do we help our youth transition to an independent adulthood with a positive life outcome?

Let's face it, it's a stark reality and one of the world's most intractable challenges, despite the widespread investment in youth initiatives. The challenge lies with how we determine what is working and how we evaluate whether youth-oriented programmes are successful when unemployment is caused largely by the structure of the economy. Does a programme result in a young person getting employed? Job placement cannot be a sole indicator of successful intervention.

Gaining momentum to make a change, or to move past inertia, is not easy. Even if on the surface the change is wanted and welcomed, old habits and mindsets die hard. But these three factors can help our youth overcome inherent challenges of change to meet their desired outcomes:

1. Young people of this generation need to know the *why*. Most people are not motivated to change unless the vision of what that change will bring is stronger and more powerful than the comfort of staying in their current state. Leaders or mentors need to paint a vision of what change will bring. Help a young person understand what will be different in the desired state. There must be emotional buy-in into the positive rewards they'll experience. Understanding our behaviour profile can be the first step towards smashing inertia.

2. Stay the course. I want to drink enough water, but I forget. I wanted to ingrain this important new habit in my life. So, I put water bottles all over my home so that I would see them and be reminded to do the thing I had promised myself I wanted to do for my own health. Leaders and mentors must expect that individuals and companies will always want to gravitate back to the old norm. Anticipate this and implement strategies to combat this natural reaction. Turn change into a game, a friendly competition, a daily conversation. Keep the change visible, talk about it frequently, and make it as engaging as possible. Even if there is a grumble, steady the course and plough on. Further down the line, momentum will kick in.
3. It takes a lifetime of discipline to change. Change and new behaviours need to become a habit. Expect setbacks, but keep practising new behaviours. Bring conscious awareness to the progress made. Eventually, the new will become the norm. Programmes are not worth much if they do not include behavioural change.

Other solutions for helping our young people take their place in the future economic market are the following:
1. Build heroes to look up to. These are heroes who have broken free of the old notions of employee/employer ideology to build resilience and mindset practices to

fight inertia and hopelessness. Let's stop training people for jobs.
2. Develop entrepreneurial mindsets. The private sector, government and education systems should collaborate to determine what knowledge and skills young people should be taught in order to find rewarding work. Businesses should play a more active role in promoting appropriate education and skills building for young people from an early age. Wider efforts to involve the private sector in education are needed.
3. Provide universal internet access and greater availability of cheap technology. Our youth should be offered the chance to self-educate in entrepreneurial skills. Computer Aid is currently providing IT education across 32 countries. This gives them access to the biggest market the world has ever had. While it's a step in the right direction, infrastructure development is a stumbling block.
4. Give the youth access to capital. Initiatives are required that will assist young people with start-up funding. They should not have to rely on banks alone, particularly since they have no credit record or steady income and will most likely be rejected. Crowdfunding sites like Youth Business International give young people all over the world the chance to get the support they need to build their enterprises and increase their income.

We should all be taking the time to help disarm the ticking time bomb of youth unemployment. The thing I know for sure is that initiative needs to go hand in hand with behavioural change. Initiative must be recognised, acknowledged and rewarded. The youth also need to feel connected or part of something that will lead to rewards and provide them with a better life outcome.

Young people should be given the right tools and the best options to make their own decisions. They must not be forced into our old way of thinking, or trained for old jobs, or told to follow in our footsteps.

THE FUTURE OF FOOD

Our diets will change, and it could all get quite weird from our current perspective. Receiving nutritional benefit while creating the volumes needed to feed billions of people will remain one of our ultimate challenges. The way we eat will be transformed, but whether it is better or worse for the planet, once again, depends on choosing with consciousness, for the collective good, and balancing science with ethics and intuition.

We are already seeing vertical agriculture, growing food in AI-controlled vertical buildings rather than on horizontal land; hydroponic plants for fruits and vegetables; and *in vitro* cloned meat. Genetically modified (GM) crops and synthetic meat are some ideas for greater food efficiency as populations continue to grow. But there is also a growing realisation that we all need a better diet, more plant-based and less reliant on processed food, to avert further illness and increased strain on healthcare systems that are still burdened with COVID-19.

Meat has less of a starring role on the menu of the future. Western culture's overemphasis on meat is just unsustainable. Meat-free diets, once a fussy, faddy choice, are now receiving interest, with celebrities bringing momentum to the movement.

I'd like to tell you my own experience here with meat-eating. Some years ago, as a result of my interaction with a dog I came to have full responsibility for quite by accident, I had a deep and unwavering understanding, for the first time in my life, of how animals are sentient beings. I wanted nothing more to do with consuming them in any way or form. My stance and my experience influenced my entire family, and we all became vegan.

During COVID, when I was staying with my parents, my father started losing his vigour right before our eyes. We could not explain it. He just seemed to be fading. One day, out of the blue, my mother decided that maybe what he needed was protein and she made him some meat. Almost instantly, his colour changed. The next day he had a bit more meat and he became stronger. He is still going strong now, and we are all now mostly vegetarian – with select bits of protein now and again.

My point here is not that we need meat. My point is that we make decisions based on what we believe is best for ourselves and the world, and increasingly we know that humans need to stop believing themselves to be gods over the earth. Slowly, we are all becoming more aware of how the literal consumption of the earth via food plays out in our kitchens.

But this story demonstrates another point too: that we cannot be rigid. That we must remain awake and alive to changing circumstances. If any of us had held on tightly to our philosophy of veganism in the face of my father's deterioration, he might not still be around. Flexibility is life. Rigidity is death.

Even so, we have a long way to go to turn the enormous ship that is the meat industry around. Livestock is responsible for about 14.8 per cent of greenhouse gas emissions and 70 per cent of global deforestation takes place to grow animal feed. Even the most committed meat eaters among us must acknowledge that continuing down the meat-guzzling path of the past is a road to nowhere for all of us.

In an article in *The Guardian*, Bruce Friedrich from the Good Food Institute predicts that by 2050, 'almost all meat will be plant-based, or cultivated'. The plant-based 'meat' burger already exists, but there could be more tempting offerings in the supply chain. Imagine sitting down to a meal of plant-based pork chops, steak, tuna or salmon? Vegan KFC, for instance, has been launched in conjunction with Beyond Meat, and it has been a runaway success.

The article goes on to say that getting consumers to buy in to cultivated or 'lab-grown' meat – developed from animal cells that are grown in a 'bioreactor', or bath of nutrients – will be challenging. At least forty companies are already working on these alternatives; Friedrich predicts that there 'won't be factory farms or abattoirs by 2050', and that, by then, our memories of this kind of food production will be like us looking back at horse-drawn carriages as a form of transport. Perhaps what may exist is a limited market of heritage breed farms where animals are treated ethically.

Food designer and futurist Chloé Rutzerveld takes it one step further and says, throw all current food theories out the window: the future of food lies in building on microorganisms. 'Instead of using growing crops or raising animals, we'll use microorganisms such as fungi, bacteria, yeast and microalgae to directly produce the carbs, proteins and fats we need,' she says in the article in *The Guardian*. Again, this will go into a bioreactor before being filtered and dried into powder. And here's the cherry on top, so to speak: it won't be like eating flavourless dust – 3D printing technology will allow us to replicate textures and flavours of regular food. Flavours and tastes will be collected on a nanoscale to recreate sensations like freshness or juiciness.

There is some controversy about this prediction. Some analysts say we can get most of the protein we need from plant-based food. If that doesn't work, we could be eating insects in 2035. Already popular in parts of the world, insects are protein-rich, low in fat and a good source of calcium. And if not eating insects directly, we can use them in the wider food chain for feeding animals. If we feed animals insects instead of crops, we can reduce deforestation.

Crops that can only be grown in very narrow climates will be at risk, like avocados, coffee and wine grapes. A one- or two-degree change in climate could make or break the regions that grow speciality crops.

I cannot talk about food without mentioning water stress. As overproduction has negatively impacted the soil in China and India, rice and wheat agriculture could be affected. Combined, these populations are expected to rise to about 3.2 billion in 2050. In countries like the UK, imported produce could become ridiculously expensive, with heavy reliance on countries vulnerable to climate change like Morocco, Spain, India and South Africa.

A problem we ignore at our peril is that the rich will continue to eat better and the diet of the poor will get worse. Dietary inequality – already evident in severe food insecurity

– is set to get worse. As soon as someone discovers a nutritious food less known in the west, they call it a superfood, hike the price and cause a knock-on effect in the areas where the food is locally consumed. Sorghum and amaranth are set to go the way of kale, quinoa and açaí berries.

As fast-food companies continue to make inroads, junk-food consumption is likely to increase, and obesity with it. Globally, 60 per cent of men and 50 per cent of women are expected to be obese by 2050 if current trends continue, according to the *International Journal of Surgery*.

If you've been eating the way you ate when you were a child, or the way you ate even five years ago, you are way behind the curve. Our concerns are no longer individual. (Am I fat? Are my arteries clogging? How can I better my time at the Comrades Marathon this year by tweaking my diet?) They have become communal and, ultimately, planetary. You might not want to try a lab-grown piece of sirloin right now, but if you haven't started doing meat-free Mondays yet, consider this your invitation to the future of your eating.

THE FUTURE OF LOVE

The internet has forever changed the way people meet and fall in love. Online dating and location-based services such as Vine, Snapchat and Grindr have opened up possibilities that allow people to look beyond their immediate friends, friends of friends and co-workers for romantic or sexual connection.

We are becoming more independent and less constrained by the old social norms. Traditional marriage setups will increasingly fade, while official and unofficial civil partnerships will continue to rise. Being single – particularly for women – is no longer seen as a sad situation, but an empoweringly happy choice. In the future, more people will remain single for longer, if not forever.

Sexualities, predilections and preferences are already increasingly coming into their own. The old, misguided, moralistic and, frankly, unnatural ideas about who could have sex with whom, when, and how are crumbling before our eyes. Polyamory – or ethical non-monogamy – might never become the choice of the masses due to its emotional, legal and practical complexities, but it will certainly no longer be a curious, secretive phenomenon.

Dr Helen Fisher, a senior research fellow at the Kinsey Institute for Research in Sex, Gender and Reproduction and an adviser to dating website Match.com, shared where she thinks relationships are heading in an article for *The Wall Street Journal*.

'Singles are ushering into vogue an extended pre-commitment stage of courtship,' she wrote. 'With hooking up, friends with benefits, and living together, they are getting to know a partner long before they tie the knot. Where marriage used to be the beginning of a partnership, it's becoming the finale.

'Any prediction of the future should take into account the unquenchable, adaptable and primordial human drive to love,' she added. 'To bond is human. This drive most likely evolved more than four million years ago, and email and computers won't stamp it out.'

Love is unlikely ever to go out of fashion or become superfluous to human needs, but the many forms it takes are being embraced more widely and openly in a world that is weary of religious moralism as a judge of whether your love has social worth.

THE FUTURE OF HEALTH

We may be getting closer to the futuristic vision with the rise of telehealth and fitness trackers, but the medical world is still full of uncertainty.

Hospitals are the costliest single element in most healthcare systems, representing up to 40 per cent of our annual health expenditure. No wonder future healthcare strategies will try to keep people out of them.

Prevention is likely to become the focus as we gain greater control of our health information, using self-monitoring biosensors and smart watches to continuously gather fitness data.

Web apps will crunch the data, syncing to electronic health records. Using these numbers, companies will be able to build a model of our overall health that can predict future problems. Being forewarned, patients will be able to take action early, changing lifestyle habits or taking designer drugs tailored to their individual DNA. This, to a large degree, is already a part of our lives, with our gym membership reporting our workout regularity to our medical aids.

If COVID has taught us anything, it's that the familiar scenario of paging through magazines in the doctor's office is fast becoming a thing of the past. Telephone and Zoom consultations have become the norm as doctors – at high risk of catching the virus from seeing several people per day – have demanded the safety of technology where it can be used.

'Telehealth platforms will make in-home patient monitoring the norm for those who need it,' says Dr Sarah Dods in a CSIRO report titled *A Digitally Enabled Health System*. Doctors will be able to consult over the internet – the perfect solution for people living in remote towns or outlying rural areas, if they are internet-equipped.

Genome mapping will lead to personalised medicines and 3D-printed replacement organs. Meanwhile, unmanned aerial vehicle (UAV) technology will be used in driverless ambulance drones. The New Zealand-based Martin Jetpack company has taken the idea of personal flying into the realm of the almost possible now (go and check out some videos on YouTube). All logistics might eventually be done by drones, once the rules and regulations have caught up. In places like New Zealand and Rwanda, they are already sending medicine and emergency goods via jetpacks or drones.

Of course, greater awareness of what we need to do to stay healthy will be equally important, as will avoiding passing health fads such as juicing, weight-loss supplements and weird detoxification rituals like eating clay. And if we can stay away from futuristic cosmetic surgery procedures such as JewelEye (implanting platinum jewels into the whites of the eye to give that movie-style sparkle), or the increasingly popular butt implants, so much the better.

THE FUTURE OF TRAVEL

Physical travel will always be on the agenda because we are primarily sensory connectors – it's an intrinsic part of our DNA. And during these times, when friends and family have been separated, it's what's keeping hope alive: the anticipation of travelling somewhere to reconnect with a person or a place or to explore something new after these years of virtual solitary confinement and what feels like domestic imprisonment. It's a case of getting vaccinated, borders opening and, where are we going and when?

I think that, as human beings, we are insatiable in wanting new experiences. And, if anything, the yearning now is greater than ever. The future of tourism is probably not as bleak as it currently feels, but will expand further and grow exponentially; as humans, we are moving towards more tailor-made experiences. Just as Stitch Fix offers a hyper-personalised clothing shopping experience in the States, or Spotify helps us tailor our music taste by analysing our preferences and suggesting musical avenues to explore, every single business, including travel agents, will be a version of this in the future. Every single business will curate, match and facilitate a designer experience for you. Clothing, shoes, sports, entertainment, music and travel. Spotify is doing a marvellous job because I listen to more music, from more creators, more often than ever before. And I don't even listen to creators any more: I listen to genres now. Even what I listen to has changed, how I listen to it has changed, everything has changed, because of Spotify.

Woolworths is doing the same thing with something as simple as cut fruit. I have never tasted oranges before like I'm tasting them now, or even seen before how they're now being sliced and diced. This is a brand-new experience – I no longer have to experience the mess of preparing pineapple or watermelon! I know I'm a brat, but as a bachelor, cutting a whole watermelon can be a waste.

Travel will become like Spotify: a unique, made-to-measure experience to satisfy every possible desire.

And you might never have to leave the comfort of your own very familiar home to voyage extravagantly. The Japan Airlines tomorrow team has spent $70 million on its 'Future of Travel department'. They've created an avatar system, a virtual reality scenario with a specially designed suit, and a number of functions that give you hot, cold, motion and direction. You can sit, for example, in your hospital bed, or on your couch, and go travelling with your grandmother on the other side of the world. The two of you can enjoy the same place and the same experiences. They've already started offering it to paraplegic people, and they're travelling everywhere from the bottom of the ocean to Jupiter. This will all fall within the ambit of the future of travel, and is happening much faster than we think.

Google has just launched a 3D platform. For the past couple of years they've been working on the most real way of communicating online, and have come up with a 3D version. It feels so real that you want to reach out and touch things. We're experiencing better and better digital experiences, and this will become part and parcel of travel.

Which is a good thing, considering how enormous your carbon footprint is when you travel by air. And no one thinking about the future can ignore the question of personal impact on the climate crisis – if not necessarily to change total carbon emissions, then at least to show concern for the planet and the consequences of decades of unbridled production without concern for the consequences of the FOMO that drives modern economies. Savvy future consumers, employers, entrepreneurs and individuals will have environmental concern as a core value, or will soon find themselves out in the cold.

THE FUTURE OF HAPPINESS

The state of global psychological misery runs counter to the message that greater digital connectivity, faster access to goods and services, and instantaneous gratification are the pathway to universal happiness. As we hurtle through the unknown towards the unknown, our reaction and adaptation to changes are having a monumental effect on our mental well-being.

The dopamine effect

Part of the issue is that in the past few decades, pleasure and happiness became confused. Pleasure is all about the phenomenon of reward. At its extreme end, it can be achieved through impulsive shopping, sex, or the kind of substance abuse that gives us a hit. Happiness, on the other hand, is a state of general contentment that requires little in the way of a trigger.

In his book *The Hacking of the American Mind*, Dr Robert Lustig explains what he calls the dopamine effect. The neurotransmitters in our brains control our pleasure/happiness responses. While the dopamine hit feels good in the moment, it suppresses serotonin, the chemical responsible for feeling calm and satisfied. Over-indulging in quick-hit pleasures has the peculiar effect of making us unhappy in the long run.

According to Lustig, too much dopamine, or a rush, makes your receptors go down to protect themselves. The consequence is that you consistently need a bigger hit for the same effect, until finally you take a huge hit with no dopamine reward. This is known as tolerance. When the neuron dies from 'a bludgeoning rather than a tickle', as he puts it, it's called addiction.

It's no longer a secret that our pleasure reactions are being carefully manipulated by big tech. Every little peek at your social media feed, every next level you reach in your game, reels you into an abusive relationship that exploits you, while also wiping out your most productive brain energy. In return, you get numbed – or at least left to feel insecure, jealous and resentful. Not a good deal, by any measure.

We're sold pleasure disguised as happiness all over the place: happy meals, happy hours, likes and comments and the fire emojis that invariably follow a selfie with your funky new glasses or haircut.

The constant approval and attention-seeking on social media can leave us vulnerable when the responses are not what we hoped. Over time, our brains become conditioned to hoping that each click will lead to bigger and better hits, or that the response will flatter our ego more.

'When I win the lottery ...'

Manipulation of our pleasure is intertwined with a skewed perception of what happiness actually is. A groundbreaking study awkwardly named 'Lottery Winners and Accident Victims: Is Happiness Relative?' tried to determine how both these groups and a control group varied in their levels of happiness. The outcomes floored the researchers.

The victims, whose accidents had rendered them either paraplegic or quadriplegic, rated themselves above average in happiness. The lottery winners were no happier than the controls, in any statistically meaningful sense. Simple pleasures like talking to friends or walking the dog had, in fact, left them *less* satisfied than before. A more comprehensive, recent Swedish study showed similar results, but with a general increase in long-term contentment among lottery winners. While the initial study was deemed crude, they both have an irresistible takeaway: money doesn't buy you happiness!

At a time when prices have increased while people have lost their jobs or taken salary cuts, this concept is a harder sell than ever. Many people are saying, 'I don't want to buy happiness. I just need a new pair of school shoes for my fourteen-year-old.'

Philip Brickman, a social psychologist, was one of the authors of this study. What makes people happy was the foundation of all his work as a researcher. He was successful in his career, had a wife and three daughters, had a brilliant wit and a fast mind, and good social connections. And yet he committed suicide by jumping of a 26-storey building when he was 38 years old.

The father of these studies on happiness was, it would seem, unable to find his own happiness. The why is unanswerable, but the context can be extrapolated. His marriage had started to unravel. He was feeling insecure in a new job, which required a skill set he lacked. His self-esteem was low and his anxiety high. Sound familiar?

The answer to his demise, oddly, could lie in his addiction to the work that preoccupied him. Happiness has little to do with cognitive processes. Rather, it has to do with matters of the heart: how we cope with adversity; how we care for others; how we form commitments, subdue inner conflict and wring meaning from this fragile, brief life.

Brickman was a perfectionist and what he did achieve he never considered good enough. He expected the same standards from others. More than anyone, perhaps, he understood that the pursuit of power, things and even happiness was futile. The more we achieve, the more we require to sustain our new levels of satisfaction, making gratification fleeting. Happiness is something which always looms *ahead*. We seldom think that we might be happy right here, in this minute.

Pleasure and happiness are not equal

Understanding the difference between pleasure (or reward) and happiness (or contentment) is the first step on the road to true happiness.

In his book, Lustig says that pleasure is the feeling of 'this feels good. I want more'. Happiness is the feeling of 'this feels good. I don't want or need any more'.

- Pleasure is short-lived, lasting only about an hour after that bar of chocolate. Happiness lasts from weeks to years.
- Pleasure is exciting and activates a fight-or-flight system, ramping up your heart rate. Happiness causes your heart rate to slow down.
- Pleasure can be achieved with different substances, such as sugar, alcohol, heroin and caffeine. Happiness cannot.
- Pleasure is 'yours and yours alone'. Conversely, our contentment or lack thereof often affects people directly and can affect society at large.
- Pleasure is associated with the act of taking, like winning

money at a casino or shopping for clothes. Happiness is often generated through giving, such as donating time or money to charity.
- Pleasure in the extreme can lead to addiction. Yet there's no such thing as being too happy.

How to find true happiness

How do we stop trying to find happiness in the very things that are sabotaging our achieving it? Where is happiness in the throes of a pandemic that hits us relentlessly with wave upon wave of grief and sorrow?

Well, dopamine and serotonin don't have to be mutually exclusive. So, Lustig suggests focusing on the four C's:

1. Connect: Anything short of face to face is not a connection. Email is not a connection, nor is FaceTime. The literal face is important because when you're interacting with someone in person your neurons adopt the emotion of that person. This generates the phenomenon we call empathy, which is necessary to produce serotonin.
2. Contribute: Contributing to something outside yourself, which is for non-personal gain, for the benefit of children, family, friends and the world at large, helps to produce serotonin. Donating money, alone, is not contributing. But you can derive happiness from work if your boss sees how the work is doing good for others and for you.

Serotonin can be boosted by helping a charity, by walking the dog, or by volunteering at a soup kitchen even just once a month.

3. Cope: This is about self-care, with sleep taking centre stage. Sleep deprivation raises cortisol levels and causes depression, which is why your sleep needs priority. Lustig calls multitasking the enemy of mindfulness. He says only 2.8 per cent of people can actually multitask. If you think you're multitasking, you're probably kidding yourself. You're really just unitasking, but going more rapidly from one thing to another. This increases stress. Exercise is recommended as an important part of coping as it tamps down cortisol.

4. Cook: This was probably the most unexpected advice for me, but cooking is considered an essential part of any happiness-focused lifestyle. If you're making your own food, you're getting fewer additives and preservatives and fresher foods that provide chemicals that support serotonin production. You will also be slowing down and engaging in one of the most precious human acts: the preparation of food to nurture mind, body *and* social relationships. Breaking bread together is one of the most ingrained and ancient ways of connecting with others and sharing humanity. I certainly noticed that it was one of the first go-to's during lockdown. Virtually

every second person was posting pictures of freshly baked bread or home-cooked meals ... because they had the time and space to (literally) feed this part of themselves.

What do we live for, if not for happiness?

How do we permanently increase the dosage of our happiness, when we live in these abnormal times? According to Brickman, *commitment* is key. Commitment may not always give pleasure; it may even oppose and conflict with freedom or happiness. But that's the point. He concluded that the more we sacrifice for something, the more value we assign to it. It could be argued that what *maintains* us is not seeking pleasure but delaying gratification. If you find happiness elusive this should make you prickle with excitement.

Commitment can also be fragile and transient, however – less fragile than the dopamine high of getting a paper published or falling in love, but still transient. Relationships end, jobs don't work out, more papers need to be written. As Brickman's apparent successes in life and marriage diminished, he began to experience the unfamiliar sensation of failure – in fact, even worse than that, it was despair. He lost his commitment, his direction and his purpose. His academic dopamine hits increased, but provided less and less gratification.

As an academic, he wrote in his last book, published

posthumously, about the following four categories of people. Tragically, Brickman would already have placed himself squarely in the fourth category.

- Those who think they're responsible for both their problems and their problems' solutions.
- Those who think they're responsible for neither.
- Those who think they're responsible for a solution to a problem, but not the problem itself.
- Those who think they're responsible for the problem, but don't have a solution.

Do we have solutions to problems we can't be held responsible for? COVID came to us. No individual sought it out, and responsibility for solving the reams of problems that came with it is a fuzzy area.

The only thing we can solve is how we choose to deal with what comes our way.

If we're going to start anywhere in our quest for happiness, let's first acknowledge the technological, reward-driven culture we've known most of our lives. We now know that to increase serotonin (happiness), we have to dampen dopamine (pleasure). That means sometimes disconnecting, something most of us have a very hard time doing. Turn off your phone for an hour a day, preferably while you have dinner with another human being. Take time out doing things that ground you, like walking the dog, cooking or meditating. Step off the treadmill of habit once in a while, eliminate your dopamine triggers, and enjoy knowing that you can control your own happiness, even in these strange times.

Positive disintegration

To move through the Anguish, familiarise ourselves with the Abnormal and – hopefully – embrace the Adventure, we have to undergo a process of positive disintegration.

For me, these two words conjure up the image of bits I no longer need falling away from me. I find it a liberating vision.

You cannot be anxious through the process of positive disintegration. It's the exact opposite. Anxiousness is holding on to outdated expectations and old versions of yourself. Positive disintegration means welcoming the de-skinning, celebrating the sloughing off of the old self.

It helps to have an outlet for the natural anxiety – which is an energy that can, after all, be harnessed to power change if you manage not to let it freeze you. I channelled all my pent-up angst and dread into exercise. Others pour themselves into hobbies.

I have begun to measure my success in new ways. My expectations have changed. Instead of worrying about the bottom line, let me engage even further with the best service providers I can find to boost my brand and keep me buoyant.

It's been a smart way for me to shift my attitude away from despair and towards joy.

And it's made me wonder: who am I becoming? Who are *we* becoming?

And where are we turning for guidance? Religion and traditional organised faith structures and modern liberalism have not guided us out of the woods here, and both have lost a lot of power as consensus about what they mean starts to cave in. People are sinking into fundamentalism, or into nihilism, or into denialism.

Collectively, if we can reach a point where we can acknowledge that things for all of us have gone horribly wrong and no one person has the answers, we can figure out how to solve this multivariable problem.

As long as we choose to bypass the human condition, our collective responsibility for how we got here, and our collective obligation towards each other, we are undermining not just the individual, but the group; not just ourselves, but a global populace.

Let's steer clear of the tired old routine of apportioning blame for this pandemic and its chaos to an entity or a collective, whether a particular nation, our government, an imagined cabal or a higher power. Feeling like you know who caused this is not going to bring you even a half a step closer to a better life, less anxiety or more happiness. So let it go. Our energy is required elsewhere, outside of the arena of finger-pointing.

When deciding to acknowledge the difficulty of the historic moment, to be in sorrow and in collective commune with a greater suffering, we're better able to respond than react. In fact, our *responsibility* is to respond, not react. It brings with it the gift of participation in a great project to help make the world better.

If you choose not to take responsibility for your state, or the process of mourning, your participation in an alternative future will be uncomfortable. We need to decolonise, democratise and participate, and weigh up how we seize the future by including people of different ages, colours, genders and cultures.

Finding meaning in the us

Millennials are poorer than their parents were at the same age. According to Dan Price – a young entrepreneur known for increasing the minimum salary of his staff to $70 000 in 2015, and decreasing his own from $1.1 million to $70 000 – millennials hold only 4.8 per cent of the world's wealth. At the same age, Gen X had 9 per cent of the wealth. Boomers had 21 per cent of the wealth.

'The largest generation in history did what the system told them to do and became the most educated in history and now, they're the poorest in history,' he said on Twitter.

Our approach should be one of reframing intergenerational and intra-human relationships. Of learning across boundaries of otherness.

Baby Boomers were not encouraged to engage with the world of emotion and developed no tools for doing so. Stiff upper lip and suppression were the order of the day. Extracting this basic and necessary component of our make-up lead to a closing down of empathy, a mindset of 'us vs them'.

The result of this is playing itself out on the global stage as the Battle of Old Men – men who have been educated and trained in a world where they are expected to divide and conquer. Think, for instance, about India and Pakistan, Israel and Palestine or China and the US. Old-school leaders with twentieth-century values, driven to beat the competition into submission to be successful. They don't understand any other way. 'I'll screw you before you screw me' was the tacit mantra of the previous century, and people who were prepared to walk over bodies to get where they wanted to go were hailed as heroic and admirable.

But a young guard is rattling the gates of power and challenging this old-man's idea of what success looks like. In the near future, we'll have automation too. All of these things are coming together to offer golden opportunities to reframe our world. From competition to collaboration. From splitting to cohesion. From exclusion to inclusion.

The rich at the top have taken all the wealth out of the system. Everything. There is nothing left for the young people coming up from the bottom. The sheer, unadulterated greed of the past half-century has benefitted a few and sold out the rest. The financial oxygen has been sucked out of the system, as quickly as carbon dioxide has been released into the atmosphere.

We are compelled to come up with new ways of creating wealth and empowering people and monetising skills that are not tradition-based. We have to question our very old-fashioned ideas about 'wealth' and 'success'.

We've already started to see this happening. The old timers own all the dollars, so the younger generation created their own economy called bitcoin. These are retaliations against older generational greed. The pandemic has forced us to face up to past failings. Let's hope it also forces us to undertake whatever we do in business, or personally, going forward with a thought spared for the generations who follow us.

Discovering authenticity

Controlling your own happiness across every sector of your life is about being honest with yourself and understanding what value you place on that.

Realness is under global scrutiny. Fake news, mistrust in politics, religion, in your own family, false friends – more and more people are just saying 'no thanks'. Perhaps it's working in pyjama pants that's made people more real, and more demanding about realness. Who knows? But there is definitely growing impatience with those who want to tell you how to think or behave, or what you need to comply with to receive your reward or punishment. We're rejecting our traditional priests and prophets, the ones who historically had the power because they could read and write – or in modern times because they were being published in mainstream newspapers or by traditional publishers.

People enter into intuitive thinking and feeling as they reject old norms and standards. Not everyone is happy about a more touchy-feely world, so don't be surprised if you come up against old-fashioned notions. Finding authenticity to offer the world something that is uniquely yours can be a perilous journey and might need you to sever some relationships or put them on pause.

When I was about twenty, I made a conscious decision to break away from the religion I had grown up in. It no longer made sense to me, and the rituals and rites just didn't fit me any more. It was a big deal for my family. I was no longer invited to religious family gatherings, which hurt me deeply, since it was also the only time I got to see my aunts and cousins. My decision to live more truly in myself removed people I cared about from my life. It's lonely to venture out into the wilderness without the protection of your family, but I needed to replenish my spirituality in a way that made sense for me. I missed the connection to my family that religion offered.

Another way in which growing into myself caused isolation from the people I cared about was when I realised, too late, that the woman I had fallen in love with was the one my mother wanted me to marry. I'd been unconsciously playing out my mother's script for me.

Moving away from religion and my marriage and, in a way, my mother's expectations of me, was very difficult, a heartsore time, but the daunting process also took me several steps closer towards my authentic self.

I lost my family for years until my mom came to watch the launch of one of my books. Time and transitions dissolved as I watched her in the first row, watching me and the person that I knew I was becoming. My mother later told me that she realised that it was only by going off script and breaking away that I was able to bring joy, love and upliftment through my books, my courses and my talks. And that I was able to do all this without following a religion.

When I broke away, it felt like I was connecting with that thing inside that's real. That only I knew and understood as my true self.

It took courage to break away from the group that had held

and nourished me all my life. You're placing yourself in an uncomfortable space. A lot of healing needs to happen for you to become authentic, and for you to forgive the ones you left behind – including the you from back then.

And, unfortunately, some cultures are much worse than others. I've lived in Dubai and the Middle East, and I'm Middle Eastern. I always say this before I say anything about the Middle East because the Middle East has a sensitive culture. Before you say anything, you have to say, 'Look, I'm part of you.' Culturally, the need to be loyal to your traditions outweighs your ability to access your genius, and that's a very unfortunate thing. You think you're happy, but you aren't, really – you're being governed by loyalty.

Right now, all the stories we carry with us are just a handful of shapes. There's the down, then the up, the rags to riches; you start out facing every disadvantage and then it all turns out well; the boy and girl meet, then they break up; they get back together and they live happily ever after. These shapes are profoundly interwoven in our lives, entrenched in western art, literature and song mythologies; theologies we are almost unaware of, but ones we go along with because they feel like truth.

The question to ask ourselves is, what narrative can work for us that can steer us in a direction that doesn't lead to sociopathic denial of our collective responsibility for one another and for this home planet of ours? We should prioritise 'self-first' principles, which place our most authentic selves at the forefront of change.

I believe that people age when they're not being themselves. It strains every aspect of your being to be something you are not. However, when you are authentic, you are in a state of flow. Things come more naturally and you operate with greater ease, reducing mental and physical strain and stress. Your perspective of time is different too. When you are lost in an activity that stimulates you, time passes differently. In my mind, living authentically is the number one anti-ageing formula. And it is where you find your genius.

What will set us apart when it comes to forging the future is grit. Grit with passion is easy and obvious. Grit with logic and loyalty is death to the self. We block access to our genius by trying to please our forefathers.

PART 3: ADVENTURE

PACKING YOUR MENTAL BAGS TOWARDS YOUR IMAGINED FUTURE

Now that we have an outline of what may be coming our way, we are on the road to being prepared for those changes.

We can stumble into the future blindfolded – which, if you've got this far in the book, you definitely aren't doing. We can reluctantly and fearfully approach it with our hands over our eyes. Or we can travel into it purposefully, looking around and anticipating exciting experiences.

The difference between these approaches is about how we decide to use our vision. 'Vision' is a word with a surprising number of meanings. Not only is it the ability to see clearly with your eyes, but it is also what you hope for and imagine, an ability to see things that others cannot, and everything you can see from a certain position or place.

A person who can predict the future is often called a 'seer'. I want to propose that everything about where we are coming from and where we are going depends on our ability to see.

Let me explain it to you like this: we need what I call HINDsight, PLAINsight, INsight and FOREsight.

HINDsight

It is useful to look back to recognise patterns, so that we can make predictions and survive in a complex world. But keeping your perspective set on the past is of ever-diminishing use in the face of a fluid future.

As a way of looking into the future, HINDsight isn't seeing at all. It's a by-product of using memories to try to plan your next step. While there's value in learning from the past, we can't hope that the approach that was relevant yesterday will be relevant today. Especially not in the realm of business. A familiar past is only ever going to offer predictable ideas that are of limited use in the unfamiliar future I laid out in the second part of this book.

PLAINsight

Experiencing the world by taking it in through our eyes and our other senses is PLAINsight. But despite our bodies' best efforts to take in the world objectively, our experiences, prejudices and circumstances influence the way in which we interpret information. Our emotional states, our biases and the way we frame things without even knowing we are framing them all affect the way we process the world. In various ways, the idea that we see things not as they are, but as we are, has come to us via various literatures and philosophies through the ages – yet we still always believe that we need only rely on what we see, without calibrating for our personal lens.

When you believe beyond doubt that 'seeing is believing'

– in other words, when you rely only on PLAINsight – you overlook the intuition, hope and faith you need to future-proof yourself. Waiting for the world to manifest in recognisable ways will only ever anchor us in the present. As quantum science challenges the validity of singular perception and suggests that – actually – *believing* is seeing, we need to realise that what we perceive is not an adequate guide for tomorrow.

INsight

INsight is where information becomes ideas. It is the recognition of a useful pattern within a set of data, and it can be incredibly powerful.

But INsight without action becomes trapped inside best intentions, or an endless cycle of analysis paralysis. When that happens, it does not drive change and is wasted. Futurist Herman Kahn talks about 'the Expert Problem' – when a person's level of education reduces their chance of seeing a solution that does not fall into the frame in which they have been taught to think.

A defiant grip on knowledge alone is not enough in an exponential reality. We need to use what we can from the past, see the world without prejudice and activate the ideas that will reveal the future.

FOREsight

When a meaningful solution to a complex problem materialises as if from thin air, when a number of insights become coherent and we can connect the invisible dots, then we can spring into coherent action.

When we can join invisible ideas and processes together in a way that suddenly makes sense of the world and offers us a clear path forward, then we have arrived at FOREsight. We can only get here by evolving through our memories, perceptions and the information that threatens to blur past us every day – and getting here is essential in the face of the future we are forging every minute of every day.

I think I can safely predict that, if what we are going to need to face what is coming next could be encapsulated in one word, that word would be 'grit'. It is a beautiful seed of a word that we all hold in the palm of our hands.

In a blog article on its website, the South African College of Applied Psychology (SACAP) says that grit is made up of five characteristics:

1. Courage, which is about sticking to your idea and backing it with all you have, doing the right thing even when it's hard, saying no, asking for help, forgiving and moving on, and staying the course.
2. Conscientiousness, which is the old-fashioned quality of caring about things and people. Being vigilant and

thoughtful and thorough, doing the best you can in what you decide to tackle. Conscientious people are principled and they stick to their convictions. They're list-makers and planners and they like orderliness.

3. Perseverance, which, says SACAP, is when you can flip your perspective on perseverance '180 degrees and view struggle as a doorway to pleasure'. It means to start and continue steadfastly towards your goal. 'Frequently, this factor alone is the difference between failure and success.'

4. Resilience, which is the ability to bounce back. People who have this quality are usually optimistic, have a sense of humour and can laugh at themselves. Like perseverance, conscientiousness and courage, resilience manifests as a determination to carry on, even when you trip up. People with resilience cultivate self-awareness and mindfulness and, instead of trying to control the outside world, they adjust to circumstances.

5. Passion, which is a deep sense of purpose. People who have it often also have the wonderful quality of enthusiasm for other people's passions and successes.

You can see how living within your authentic, self-aware self will support your latent grittiness. But, on top of cultivating grit, I want to suggest that one of the most important things you can do for yourself – for every aspect of your life – is to teach yourself to unlearn.

'The more expert – or at least the more educated – a person is, the less likely that person is to see a solution when it is not within the framework in which he or she was taught to think,' says Herman Kahn in a Hudson Institute article.

The adventure that is the future isn't going to be here tomorrow, and that gives me some solace – it gives me an opportunity to understand how I need to go about accessing the deepest parts of myself so that I can continue to develop my purpose.

PURPOSE IS AN EQUATION

For me, purpose is an equation.

> Purpose = Wisdom + Reframing + Curiosity + Intuition + Entrepreneurship + The business of you + Money frequency

You might have your own equation, or a different definition of what you think your purpose is, but I'd like to share with you some of my stories and suggestions as I have tweaked this equation over the past fifteen years of working on myself.

Wisdom

'Wisdom is having memories with no triggers.'
– *Joe Dispenza*

'The knowledgeable man has to learn something new every day, but the wise man has to unlearn something new every day.' – *Alan Watts*

Both of these quotes, which have framed my own understanding of wisdom, reflect an unspoken directive: heal your past.

If you heal your past, you heal your future.

In this context, wisdom for me is making peace with the past, with myself and with the antagonists that have crossed my path – and to view all three as teachers. I did this with the man who helped me go bankrupt when I was 30. I did this with my father when I turned 40 and was tired of being angry with him. I did this with the ex-girlfriend who cheated on me.

All three took up far too much of my thinking, for far too long, I'm sad to admit. But I slowly came to realise that, because of the things that had happened between me and them, I'd had some profound revelations. Each had been a catalyst for some groundbreaking new thinking.

Understanding this made me feel lighter, and wiser too.

When I got to that part of dealing with my pain, I realised that I had tamed the experiences into 'memories with no triggers'. We can be addicted to our triggers because they are familiar. What is unknown is always scarier and less comfortable than what is known, even when what is known causes you grief.

The other thing about situations or people or memories that spark a lot of unwelcome feelings is that those things are actually a useful point of focus. Focus is the engine of consciousness. Training your focus on what repeatedly makes you blow a gasket means getting to the root of an important lesson your unconscious is trying to teach you. You are probably only going to be able to do this if you allow yourself the silence, the time and the space in which to investigate it. Remember, a body of water can only reflect the environment when its surface is calm. You will only find the wider truth when you allow yourself to feel your feelings in peace and think about them in quiet.

I figure, now, that if I haven't forgiven someone from my past, it means I am more connected to the identity I currently cling to than to the identity I could have.

Mostly, we are all – circumstances allowing – fantastically courageous by nature. All around us, during this pandemic, we have seen people rise, and keep rising – and, alongside all the sadness of the past couple of years, we have been amazed at human resilience and resourcefulness. By rebooting our lives over and over while we help one another hold on and hold up, through radical hope and by learning to unlearn, we have shown ourselves to be able to survive crushing pain, disappointment and sorrow. We have accepted the messy, ineffable mystery of being alive, even if we haven't quite yet integrated it all. And for that, we need the second thing in the purpose equation.

Reframing

Everyone has a series of 'filters' in their perception through which they frame the world. These filters are built from various influences, which can be biological, cultural and even linguistic. We use these filters to make sense of the world, and the choices we make are influenced by the frames we create. Framing is the way in which we interpret the world. Without even realising it, the way we understand and respond to events is based on the unique collection of stereotypes and anecdotes we carry around inside ourselves.

I – and the rest of my family – had to reframe our ideas about eating animals when we were watching my dad fade away and were feeling afraid, for example. We hadn't realised how badly he needed meat in his diet.

We frame the world so deeply in our subconscious that we often find it impossible to think about totally reframing how we see the world. Imagine reframing the relationship between

China and America to one of friendship. Imagine how the fate of humankind could be changed if these two superpowers, backed by their collective reserves of brain power, framed themselves as friends and not enemies! Sadly, both are run by a generation that operates on the principle of competition rather than collaboration, and are exploiting and depleting finite resources we all need instead of opting to plug into the infinite resource of creative association.

In order to reframe, though, we have to heal the past. For me, the reframing of my relationship with men in general – starting with the man who helped me go bankrupt, and forgiving my father for my childhood and my upbringing – has reframed my perspective of masculinity. Instead of seeing men as antagonists, as I did for many years, I now approach them as friends, and I look forward to building even stronger brotherhoods with them. Negative experiences of masculinity framed my perception of men. My conscious decision has been to reframe my picture, to turn men from adversaries to allies in my own mind.

Reframing on a global scale

To reframe means to take the same data and to assemble it differently. Framing explains how we can interact with one other and come up with solutions.

There are so many examples on a global political scale of

framing issues, such that entire nations or groups of people are set up as either strategic competitor or enemy.

Here's another example of how framing works. In the early days of the pandemic, the UK and US pronounced COVID to be seasonal flu, and they mitigated it with basic steps. In countries like Taiwan, South Korea, New Zealand and Australia, the looming crisis was framed on the mental model of SARS and not seasonal flu. They threw everything they had at the problem. And they did much better at containing the virus, although some might argue that they overreacted.

Countries have had some time, now, to stop thinking about reacting to the problem and start thinking about how to react to major crises in the future. We hope they are taking measures that include reframing their approach to disaster. It took trillions to support the economy when the first wave hit. We could have spent millions in preventative measures before the disaster landed. 'How can we reframe our apprehension of disaster better?' is the question I hope leaders are asking themselves. Finland and Norway, for instance, have an emergency response programme that is viable in any situation.

Kenneth Cukier, author and award-winning journalist with *The Economist*, explains that a frame is a point of view through which we view every decision we make. Models, templates and patterns in our brain help us make sense of the world, and we use them navigate it. For that reason, it's hard to 'think outside the box', as businesses often tell their employees to do.

Instead of trying to think outside the box, people should understand that box (or frame) and try to grasp how it limits the options we can see. Then, they need to adjust those frames with additional points of view. We can do this by considering the following:

1. Causality: How is the world working? What is the cause or effect? What are the predictable outcomes?
2. Counter-factual: How do I respond to the 'what if' in this world?
3. Constraints: What am I focusing on at the exclusion of something else?

Curiosity

Curiosity is an invisible, effervescent energy source that we access when we do things we are intensely excited about or that we are fascinated by. When we are led through inquisitiveness to some activity we lose our sense of time, falling into a unique vibrational connection with our own vitality.

About five years ago, I made a decision that I wanted only to do things that excited me. I realised that the things that did not excite me were the things I wasn't very good at. The things I was good at were the things I was curious about.

From a very early stage in my speaking career, I started hiring more and more people around me and, compared to my contemporaries, spending much more on them. I then delegated all the things I wasn't very good at. I believe that my career has been incredibly successful because of this. Leaping into doing only what I was curious about, and spending the money before I had achieved success just to give myself the time to think, fed my endeavours generously. Immersing myself in my curiosity and giving myself permission and the freedom to do what I excel at, rather than getting caught up in the nitty-gritty that drains me, has allowed me to write five books in five years, and speak to audiences around the world.

Curiosity provides the highest excitement with the lowest expectation of outcomes, liberating you in ways you cannot even begin to imagine until you've tried it. Pursuing it is energising.

Curiosity will also help you connect with and possibly monetise your passion, if that is what you desire to do. Most important, though, is that it allows you to access your own personal genius. Remember that genius is not some rare thing that some people were just lucky enough to get. Genius is defined as any exceptional intellectual or creative power or other natural ability. It's the ability to create, imagine or think in new ways. The Romans had this idea that we all had a pocket of genius located just above us from the minute we were born to the time we died, and that it was our job to access it. And if the two most important days of your life are the day you were born on and the day you find out why, then the way to get to that second day – which is when your genius is born – is through curiosity.

If you're wondering why you need to access your genius at all, just think about where you currently are. Do you love your life and what you do? Or are you hammering away at the same old thing, dragging yourself from one task to the next, until you collapse in depletion at the end of the day? Might there be another way to end the day: not fatigued and exhausted, but amped and joyful and happily tired?

When you've tapped into the creative genius you were born with and you're using it, you've become aligned with your purpose. There is no tedium in that.

With all the noise surrounding us, and all the demands and stresses of daily life, how do we allow ourselves the luxury of harnessing this genius? Well, I try dispensing with logic and accessing my heart to help gain access to my intuition. Practise this and you'll have pure, solid gold. Also, stop wasting that energy and start saying no to the things that fail to add meaning or value to your well-being. If it does not feed your genius, it's stealing from it.

A good example of curiosity and leveraging genius is the Disney company. By staying true to curiosity as a value key, Disney embarked on a phenomenal growth trajectory, from being worth $6 million in 1950 to having a market cap of more than $238 billion in 2020, with interests spanning the globe. The Disney brand remained close to the vision of the man after whom it was named, and it remains dedicated to innovation. It was Walt Disney's genius that laid the groundwork for the company to become the media giant it is today.

Now, let's take it one step further. For our genius to truly flourish, mix up obsession with *still* space. Short periods of super-focused and intense thinking followed by spurts of quiet and space allow us to connect the invisible dots and access our genius. And the idea of accessing our genius is to weave it through the genius of others – improving general wellbeing and making the world a better place for us all to live and thrive in.

Intuition

When you can combine wisdom, framing and curiosity as quickly as possible so that it becomes automatic, and your adaptability quotient is on fire so you're able to perceive, conceive and act quickly – and you become fit at it – it becomes intuition.

Intuition is when you're following this incredible mix of excitement, ease about your past and continuous reframing of your life, and you're being led by something other than yourself. This is where you want to be to maximise your entrepreneurial opportunities and develop the most authentic version of yourself and your business.

Adaptive quotient (AQ) vs intelligence quotient (IQ)

The first way people began to try to measure ability was by using intelligence quotient (IQ) testing, now a disputed and controversial method that has some murky history in eugenics – on top of which, it turns out not to be a predictor of success. Then, in the mid-nineties, author Daniel Goleman introduced the idea of emotional intelligence (EQ). This is the ability to understand, use and manage your emotions in positive ways.

Now, Amin Toufani, a businessman and founder of the Adaptability University, is showing us that the greatest predictor of success is, in fact, the ability to adapt to change. He calls this adaptive intelligence (AQ), which is made up of three components: perception (you need to receive the information), conception (you need to make sense of the world), and action (you need to do something).

When Google bought YouTube, which at the time had no other real takers, it used adaptive intelligence. YouTube had no profits, its core business had nothing to do with Google's core business and, on top of that, it was locked into some legal troubles. But Google noticed YouTube's traffic accelerating (perception), worked out what this might mean for the future (conception) and purchased it (action).

The difference between IQ and AQ is that AQ has shown itself to be highly teachable. To learn it:

- We can challenge our ability to take information in by *amplifying perceptions*. Usually, when we see something that doesn't fit the pattern or that challenges our common understanding, we tend to push it aside or to the back of our minds. The first thing we, or our organisation, has to do is allow ourselves to pause and amplify the things that want to slip away from our perception because they don't fit into what we know of the world. Here, it helps to have more people perceiving together to show one another those things that we aren't seeing ourselves.
- We can share *conceptions* of the world. Ideas about how the world works are different from brain to brain, each with its own blind spots or brilliant insights. Create a safe environment around you, in which people feel comfortable about sharing their conceptions of the world.
- We can reward the *actions* people take and not their achievements. If you only reward achievements, you're going to discourage experimentation because it creates a fear of failure. The same applies to yourself. When something new you try doesn't work, be glad you tried; don't dump on yourself because you failed.

To get this kind of adaptive intelligence going in an organisation, make sure that you are surrounded by as much diversity as possible. The more people with more diverse ideas about the world you come into contact with, the more informed and prepared you are – never mind the incredible benefits of exposure and experience and growing empathy.

Toufani suggests bringing in the people who are known to have weird ways of doing things and listening to them. He also says we should all have 'knowledge of a lack of knowledge'. If there is a circle around us demarcating the stuff we know, and beyond that circle is all the stuff we don't know, then the border of the circle represents the questions that connect the inside and outside of that circle. The problem, though, is that saying you don't know is often seen as uncool. You have to get comfortable with knowing that the unknown exists and heading towards it.

Another way to put this might be just not to be arrogant. No matter who you are, how far you've come, what you've come through, who you know, how much you earn, or who your friends are, you do not know everything. People with high adaptability are able to ask the questions others don't want to for fear of looking weaker or less knowledgeable than their peers.

Which brings us right back to the question of unlearning. While everyone seeks stability for themselves and their businesses, and wants to keep doing what they've always done, it is has been shown that businesses that are prepared to unlearn are more stable. Changing – taking the risk of following the intuition you have developed from the combination of your knowledge and experience – is particularly hard when you are already successful at what you do. So, even if people acknowledge that unlearning is the way to future-proof yourself, a cost-benefit analysis might cause anyone to retreat, because intuition and unlearning bring fear with them. Innovation and change are high-risk. You have to find ways to balance the fear of unlearning how you do what you do with the possibilities that doing things differently brings.

Toufani says there is one simple question to ask yourself when fear is holding you back: 'One year from today, which project will I regret not starting?'

Working intuitively requires knowledge of your field, yes, but it also requires a bit of a leap, a bit of letting go, a lot of trust in yourself and the people who surround you, a bit of motivating fear, empathy and courage.

It's not an easy sell, but it is a deeply satisfying way to work.

Entrepreneurship

We are entering, I believe, the era of forced entrepreneurship. Most people in recent decades have believed that the route to career success was to study, get an internship and find a cracking job. But that's getting harder to do, and perhaps even less desirable.

Forced entrepreneurs are people who have no initial

intention to start their own businesses, but who are forced by circumstances to strike out on their own. But forced entrepreneurship doesn't have to imply starting something new outside of what you're currently doing. Within the realm you are already in, there are opportunities for continued problem-solving without a loss of enthusiasm. In fact, if you're wired for puzzles and can not just understand but also celebrate the struggles, you're forging entrepreneurship inside your current reality. You're keeping things fresh and finding that there are multiple routes to purpose. With the internet it has never been easier to sell products and services, with gatekeepers out of the way. So, it's up to us to show up, hire the right people, follow our highest excitement and bring about maximum impact.

Abraham Lincoln famously said that 'the best way to predict your future is to create it'. Young people are, almost by definition, more creative, energetic and enthusiastic than people in their thirties and beyond. They have a grasp of technology that we can never hope to have unless we've been working in tech. They hold the solutions to so many problems, but if they are only allowed to explore those solutions within companies that are loath to give them time for experimentation, or at home where they don't have access to the kind of financial support required for research and development, then potential fixes are just sliding by us at a rate of knots.

Youth entrepreneurship is a beacon of hope around the world. With so many challenges stemming from ineffective governance, lack of infrastructure and lack of funding, being a young entrepreneur requires perseverance, networking and passion. Since most socioeconomic support efforts have been decimated by the COVID-19 pandemic, how do we harness youth start-ups and use them as levers to rebuild a sustainable SME sector?

How do we cultivate an entrepreneurial mindset among the youth through non-formal education? Should education systems be reshaped to connect young people with the job market? Educational facilities are failing to equip people with the skills they need, such as digital literacy, general business acumen and other soft skills like confidence, communication and problem-solving aptitude.

Interestingly, volunteerism can lead to youth entrepreneurship. It provides access to civic groups and social networks, and connects young people with resources and information. It also offers access to mentors, partners and funding.

Taking this all into account, youth entrepreneurship must move further up on the agendas of global leaders, with legal frameworks for protection and tax incentives for start-ups. We need the media to make a bigger deal out of people who have broken out of the poverty cycle, to give us all heroes to look up to. Governments should give away more data infrastructure to everyone. And we, as a society, need to be educating ourselves about internet-based entrepreneurship that focuses not only on local, or national, but global possibilities.

Without a doubt, the time for young people to ward off uncertainty and build their future has arrived.

As we move into this era of forced entrepreneurship, development of the personal or individual brand has also taken on value. As important as building a business is building the business of you.

The business of you

To declare ownership of an animal, farmers sear the rump of their livestock with their own unique hot iron. As an animal lover, I find the infliction of pain on animals hard to stomach. But the word 'brand' has stuck and developed in the past hundred years or so to mean the public declaration of representation by an individual, a company or a business.

When the world plunged into murky uncertainty, the distinction between the personal and the corporate in professional identity became hazy and blurred, as in the most obvious case of individual footballers having more followers than the clubs they belong to. The personal brand is now bigger than the collective brand, and more and more people are becoming player fans than team fans. This is true for personal brands too. We trust humans over corporate brands.

This is what the passion economy is about. I truly believe the world will move increasingly towards it as we see the benefits in it: how we work, the lifestyles we lead and the money we can make with very few overheads, and not being pinned anywhere geographically.

The sooner we can move away from the stressors of staff and offices, and move into our own space and develop our own personal brand, the sooner we will become independent and autonomous. That is incredibly powerful.

This can be done as an individual, as well as within an organisation. If you are working in an organisation and you're enjoying it, that's also great. The world needs progressive organisations that do great things, like Amazon and Apple. Your personal brand is as important there as if you were striking out on your own. The way we develop personal brands is through thought leadership, unique storytelling and authenticity.

When you can be authentic, and be a great storyteller, and you're able to do this with cadence, as often as possible, sharing your thought leadership positions you very powerfully. For me, my personal brand is obviously what I build on – that's why I try to write a book every year and do podcasts, talks, marketing and public relations. And I'm always reading, researching and sharing with everybody.

The simplest and clearest way to market yourself as a

personal brand, after you've discovered your genius, is by sharing your work and how you relate to it. Many entrepreneurs hesitate to share themselves personally for fear of putting off potential customers. We want to be liked by everyone, so we often fail to be our authentic selves for fear of rejection that will lose us potential clients. But the truth is that by taking a stand, you create superfans and release the lukewarm ones to find what they need elsewhere. It's often the alignment of values and resonance with stories that endear us to brands and influence our buying decisions. As life coach Andrea Leda says, 'I don't share my wounds, but I do share the wisdom of my wounds.'

Think about how you relate to friends and family who have personal brands. People feel obligated to like people, but are often ambivalent about liking businesses. Studies have shown that when identical messages are shared on personal social media accounts and business brand accounts, they are shared an average of 24 times more. So, this is about marketing yourself.

What about monetising yourself?

Aligning yourself with the money frequency

So many of us are bonded to our idea of what wealth is – even though it isn't working for us or the planet – because of the very nature of our relationship with money. We expect money to fulfil our fantasies, calm our fears, ease our pain and send us soaring to heights of gratification. In fact, we are programmed to think that money can fulfil most of our wants and desires. We want to be able to buy *everything*, from hair implants to hope, from a Hermès watch to happiness. We don't *live* life, we *consume* it.

Transforming our relationship with money and re-evaluating our emotional frequency patterns around it could put us and the planet back on track. We need to learn from our past, gain clarity about our present and create a new, reality-based relationship with money, discarding assumptions that don't work.

How do we do that? By altering our money frequency. To attract what we want in life, we must find joy in that thing.

If you are in your forties or older and come from an average background, it is quite likely that you were brought up by parents who'd inherited the post-war mentality of scrimping and saving and worrying that there's not enough to go around. If you went to school with children who seemed to come from wealthy backgrounds, while your mother was busting a gut to pay your school fees on her tiny salary, you will have an ingrained sense of lack and perhaps an exaggerated idea about what money can do for you. Or perhaps you grew up in a family where you were told to eat everything on your plate, because there were poor children out there who had nothing.

We adopt all sorts of narratives from our religions, cultures and parents that are aligned with a shortage mindset and influence the way we feel about money as adults.

And while, for many, 'more money' might have just been a dream you kept pursuing so you could buy the clothing brands you love or go an overseas holiday, the real power of money over our emotions became a lot more real in 2020. Money is deeply linked to a sense of existential security. COVID-19 gave every single one of us a taste of the visceral fear of financial insecurity.

But if you're feeling that money has become elusive and fraught with deep worry, you're possibly repelling the financial state you're trying to acquire. It requires discipline to relearn how we respond to the energy of money.

THE BEGINNING OF A NEW ROAD MAP FOR MONEY

Using the word 'relationship' in a sentence with money may sound odd, because money is not a person, it's a thing. True, but we are choosing to trade our life energy for it. We are giving energy to what we're doing so we can earn money and then use it. That's why money sparks reactions like fear, guilt and avoidance, dread and panic. So, while money does not breathe, our life energy does. It would be great if we could tweak our life energy to react to money with joy and a sense of abundance. Money is, in essence, a neutral thing: it is we who give it vitality with the energy we send towards it.

My experience is that there are things I can do to break habitual thinking that constrains or distorts my relationship with money.

- I can focus on what I have instead of what I do not have, or what I have lost, simply because nothing comes from constantly going over what is lacking.
- I can purge myself of envy. In the past, even when I'd noted what I had and been actively grateful for it, I'd find myself sitting with envy when I'd see what others had. And it could really gnaw at me, even though I wanted for very little. Then I realised that my jealousy projects an inaccurate narrative on others that has more to do with me than it has to do with their perceived wealth. Envy has not served me in inviting abundance. It has merely narrowed and restricted me, the opposite of abundance.
- I can educate myself. Sadly, understanding money is not a basic school subject and it really should be. We get let out into the world with zero information about how to manage our money. We need to be able not only to see to our basic needs, but also to save and invest for the future and even contribute to making the world a better place. Not knowing makes you fundamentally unable to

operate with confidence. Whatever you know about how money works, you can always learn more.

- I can go further than just knowing how money and markets work. I can actively study how wealth is accumulated. How have people who've succeeded done it? What are their habits and practices? But beware of thinking that it's only flashy people who are wealthy. Many people who are way more than comfortable do not live flashy lives – and often that is part of the reason for their financial security.
- I can ask myself, do I want to have money so that people can see I'm doing well? Or do I want to have money so that I can have a strong sense of security in the world in order to do the strong, innovative, creative and satisfying work that I am called to do during my time on earth?
- I can respect my money, which is the fruit of my labour and hard work. That means that I care for it in a loving – not avaricious or greedy – way, by keeping track of it. I can recognise its ability to do good and its ability to perpetuate cruel systems. I can invest my money in things and companies and people that are making the world better, not stripping the planet or animals or other human beings of life and of dignity.
- For abundance to thrive, I can teach myself to invest in projects that I believe can bring about much goodness

in the world. There is a spiritual aspect to giving both time and money that will improve my life ten times more than simply holding on to everything I earn for myself and for my family.

There are ways in which we can change our emotions towards and relationship with money.

Money requires purpose. We need to give instructions and directions to the energy of money, much like giving ourselves GPS coordinates to reach a destination. I retrained my brain and emotions to give direction and capacity to where my money should be going.

Money flow requires cadence. How much money do you want to make and what do you need it for? How often do you want to make money and how does that fit in with the rhythms of rest and relaxation in your life? How do you interact and transact with your money? What is your biggest dream for yourself and your money? Intention, together with clarity, creates a good flow with money.

Money requires a mental container. What does the mental vessel you hold for your income to pay for your basic needs and comforts look like? Is it a swimming pool or a goldfish bowl? It is porous, like a sieve, or built from solid concrete? And is it independent from crippling financial beliefs, debt and an inability to manage modern conveniences?

If the daily grind is making us happy, its sacrifices and inconveniences would be worthwhile. But for most people that's not the case. Everyone, regardless of what they're doing or how much they earn, can become financially fit and transform their money health radically. Don't be afraid to ask people to assist you with this shift. Get help, read books, watch videos, get a coach.

I went on a money course. I had a coach for three years, just talking about money and how and where it flows in my life. I followed abundance meditations. It's all about a frequency shift, away from the stories we used to tell ourselves about ourselves and our money and towards a space where we can create new ideas and attract the money that will elevate us to a state of joy.

Joy is more than happiness. It's made up of three states: excitement, ease and love. Almost like a real relationship.

FINDING PURPOSE IN WHO WE BECOME

The past few years have upended so many dreams, so many secure ideas we have had about ourselves and the world and the people in our lives.

I don't know whether we will be able to grasp the full extent of the anguish we've endured, or the depth of our perplexity about the abnormality of our new world, or the loss of what used to feel like a problematic but at least familiar world, or the unimaginability of the adventure that is the future. The upheavals we've faced and discomfort we've felt aren't over yet; what's certain is that we'll need to face the discomfort of this strange new world of ours with optimism through struggle.

None of us knows where the adventure will take us, but one thing I do know is that I cannot try to carry the heavy luggage of old patterns and comfort zones and ideas into the future. They did what they needed to do at a time when I needed them. I thank them. And I let them go.

I thank my past self, my past struggles, my difficult teachers, my mistakes and my courage. I thank my past successes.

I honour my confusion.

I honour the hopelessness and fear I felt, especially during that first hard lockdown.

I see my sadness and I hold it.

I allow myself to grieve for the things I had to put off, the dreams I had to delay, the relationships I lost, the people who died. I let in all the feelings.

I cry.

I run or cycle to get rid of the frustration and to remember that I am lucky enough to have a body that carries me from yesterday towards tomorrow.

I know that emotions are useful and that, if I just let them come to me, without cowering or dodging, they will not kill me. So, I let them march through me, one by one, and I acknowledge them and give them space in which to live fully, because I know that they then become less threatening to me.

I teach myself that while I hunger for learning, I must remember also to unlearn something every single day.

I do not know what my long-terms plans are, but I'm using this vacuum in time created by the pandemic to experiment with various aspects of myself and my business until I find my authentic self to take into an uncertain future. And I keep asking:

Who do I become?
Who do *you* become?
Who do *we* become?

ABOUT THE AUTHOR

John Sanei is a global speaker, future strategist and trend specialist, who combines human behaviour and future studies to create keynotes, masterclasses and books that help people, businesses and brands build the courage and clarity they need to forge the future they want. Sanei has brought his dynamic message to corporates and individuals across the world. He divides his time between South Africa, the United Arab Emirates and the UK.